GHOSTS & LEGENDS OF LICKING COUNTY

GHOSTS & LEGENDS OF LICKING COUNTY

NOVA STILES

Haunted America

Published by Haunted America
A Division of The History Press
Charleston, SC
www.historypress.com

All images by author unless otherwise noted.

Cover image: *Sad Angel* statue in Cedar Hills Cemetery.

First published 2022

Manufactured in the United States

ISBN 9781467152013

Library of Congress Control Number: 2022933414

Notice: The information in this book is true and complete to the best of our knowledge. It is offered without guarantee on the part of the author or The History Press. The author and The History Press disclaim all liability in connection with the use of this book.

CONTENTS

Introduction

The Dark History of Licking County, Ohio

Licking County, Ohio, named after the Licking River that flows through it, was created on January 30, 1808. The European immigrants who settled the area were mostly of German, English and French descent. Before the Europeans arrived, the land was home to a number of Native American tribes. One of the first groups of people that can be traced back to what we now know as Licking County is the Hopewell tribe. The Hopewells carved and shaped beautiful patterns, designs and symbols into the ground to form land art known as earthworks. These works of art had religious or sentimental meaning to many of the Hopewells, and it is believed that the earthworks were created as a place to perform religious or cultural ceremonies and burials or to study astronomy.

When the Europeans moved onto the land, they tore up most of these earthworks to create space to build homes and farms. Although a few of these works of art remain today and are kept preserved by local governments and historical societies, the majority of them have been destroyed. The Hopewell people had strong emotional ties to the earthworks and were very upset with the destruction of the sacred ground. Today, at least three of the remaining earthworks are said to be haunted, and it is rumored that the spirits of Hopewell warriors guard the last bit of earthworks that remain. Tourists and visitors have had orbs appear in photos they take of the works of art, and some guests have even been able to see orbs or apparitions of native spirits with their own eyes. Other ghostly reports have included hushed whispering, disembodied male voices, the smell of pipe smoke when no source of it can be found and drumming music being played at night.

Newark, named after the city in New Jersey, was founded and became the county seat in the early 1800s. English settlers Samuel Parr and Samuel Elliot became the very first residents of the area when they built their log cabins in 1802. As more families moved into the area and established a neighborhood, Licking County's first courthouse was established in 1808. Over the following few decades, the county continued to expand. The Ohio Canal was created in July 1825, and the Sandusky, Mansfield, Newark Railroad was finished in 1852; their construction helped bring more settlers into the area to buy property and raise a family. What really helped this area of Ohio grow was an act that was passed after the Revolutionary War. The government wasn't able to pay for all the salaries of the soldiers who fought for liberation, so Congress decided to make up the compensation by giving the veterans land in Ohio. Through this Congressional act, most of the foliage that once stood was turned into neighborhoods.

To the west of Newark, just before you reach Ohio's state capital, sits another one of the most populated cities in the center of the state, Pataskala, Ohio. One of the first settlers in the area was a man named Richard Connie, who arrived with his wife in 1805. He purchased two thousand acres of land and began building homes and farms in order to form a village that he named Connie in 1821. Thirty years later, in 1851, the area was renamed to Pataskala, the term that the local Native Americans had for the Licking River. The area continued to grow in population with the help of industrialization as well as the large influx in German immigration. In the early 1990s, Pataskala was granted its city status.

Soon after the village of Connie was created, the local church organizations came together to discuss burial practices for the new area. The union congregation of the Lutheran Church and the reformed churches came together to establish the first official burial ground for the newly settled area. By 1847, the congregation had successfully established St. Jacobs Church Cemetery. As some of the first bodies began being buried in the cemetery and the grounds began forming their design, the early settlers began to notice strange behavior.

As villagers would pass by the cemetery late at night, they would hear the sound of children singing among the headstones. Some would even report seeing shadowy, childlike figures running about and playing. Due to the fact that most of the immigrants in the area were of German descent, the haunting was given the name "Kinder der Nacht," which translates in English to "Children of the Night." The church congregation went through the cemetery with holy water and read scripture in an attempt to bless and purify the area, but the reports of the children continued. After the failed cleansing, some members of the community refused to bury their loved ones at St. Jacobs because they believed that the area was cursed or demonic.

The county continued to grow and inhabit more and more of the land that was once called home by the Hopewell tribes. Even though the Hopewells were either killed or forcefully relocated off the land, they were not the only ones to have their blood spilled here. Despite Ohio being the light at the end of the tunnel for slaves escaping through the Underground Railroad, they still faced racism and discrimination in the North. Abolitionists would try to safeguard the freed slaves in areas like Columbus and Cincinnati, where some of the trails of the railroad ended, but groups of lynch mobs were formed by white supremacists and slave masters to punish escapees. Lynching was prominent all throughout this section of Ohio.

The number of famous lynchings in Ohio is quite shocking. One of the most famous in Licking County took place in 1910. During Prohibition, the city of Newark became a "dry" city. Despite the majority of the population voting against legislation to ban the sale of alcohol, prohibitionists protested and forced the closing of seventy-eight bars and saloons in the area. One day, a seventeen-year-old anti-saloon detective by the name of Carl Etherington was scouting the Charles Henry Saloon. While looking for an excuse to close the saloon permanently, the owners and bar patrons learned of the true nature of his visit.

The crowd of customers quickly turned into an angry mob and swarmed around Carl to attack him. While being beaten nearly to death, Carl panicked

The Licking County Courthouse sits right in the heart of Newark Square, where Carl Etherington was lynched by angry citizens.

and fired his weapon into the crowd. The bullet hit and mortally wounded William Howard, a respected retired police officer of the town. The police managed to save Carl from the crowd but proceeded to take him to Licking County Jail for the murder. Despite being behind stone walls and iron bars, Carl was still not safe from the rage of the town. The mob grew as word of the murder spread throughout the city. The crowd stormed the jail and dragged Carl out into the street. He was beaten with a hammer and publicly hanged in the town square.

Murder seemed to have a home in Licking County, as it also birthed two of the state's most famous serial killers in the late 1970s. Two brothers, Gary and Thaddeus Lewingdon, began a murderous spree in December 1977 that took the lives of residents of Licking County, as well as in Franklin and Fairfield Counties. The elder brother, Thaddeus, was a graduate of the Cleveland Institute of Electronics. He worked a respectable job at the Columbus Steel Drum Company. Gary was a veteran of the Vietnam War and retired from the U.S. Air Force. Both men were married, and Thaddeus had fathered three children. They were looked at as outstanding members of society and had completely normal and honorable lives. It came as a complete shock when it was discovered that the two men were capable of committing such diabolical crimes.

The killing spree began in Newark, outside Forker's Café. The Lewingdon brothers attacked Joyce Vermillion and Karen Dodrill as the women were exiting the bar to return home for the night. The women were shot, and their bodies were looted of all the money and valuables they had. They had done nothing to provoke Gary and Thaddeus. The brothers had chosen these women as victims simply because they were strangers who lived far away from where the brothers lived, and there were no witnesses around at the time of them leaving the bar. They were seen as easy targets, with no way of having the murders traced back to them. Soon after that, they invaded a home in Franklin County and took the lives of homeowners Robert and Dorothy McCann as well as their houseguest, Christine Herdman. Each victim was shot several times in the head. A few months later, they went to Granville, Ohio, and took the life of Jenkins Jones as well as his four dogs. After each killing, the twisted brothers looted all money and valuables from the homes of the deceased.

Gary and Thaddeus continued to break into residences and murder the occupants together, in addition to killing a security guard at a local club, throughout the year. One night, Gary attempted to commit a murder of his own without the help of his accomplice. He successfully took the life of Joseph Annick, a resident of Columbus, but was caught after using the victim's credit card at the local department store. Through the questioning of Gary, the police uncovered the whole operation and brought Thaddeus into custody as well. The police searched both of their homes and uncovered the murder weapons, which they were able to link to the scene of the crimes by comparing the firearms to the casings left behind at the murders. The police also took the brothers' fingerprints and compared them to the ones left at the crime scene. Of course, the fingerprints matched. Ten murder cases were tied to these men, and they were given multiple life sentences.

Gary did not adapt well to prison life. He was acting up and ignoring orders from the guards. He always tried to get in with the gangs for protection, but to no avail. After a while, he began to show warning signs of suicidal ideation. After being examined by professionals, he was moved to Lima State Hospital to receive treatment and placed on a closer watch. Gary was a problem at this facility as well and even attempted to escape in 1982. Thaddeus, on the other hand, was tamer and more well behaved. He admitted that his participation was due to his financial struggles. He claimed that he was doing what he did for his family and that Gary had used that as leverage to coerce him into assisting in the crimes. Thaddeus eventually passed away in jail, after succumbing to lung cancer in 1989. Gary took his own life in 2004 while still in custody.

Since before the founding of this county and the cities within it, there has been bloodshed and evil across the land. From the tragedy of the Hopewell tribes to the lynchings of escaped slaves and Carl Etherington, to the murders and fear brought about by the Lewingdon brothers, a dark cloud seems to hang over Licking County. Every town in this part of Ohio has its own stories and urban legends to be shared by the residents, and most of them have recorded history to provide some insight as to where the stories originated. The chapters of this book will tell the stories of the real-life events that led to the most famous hauntings of the area, as well as the myths and urban legends that are told by the locals. Whether you are a paranormal enthusiast, a true crime fan local to the area or a history nerd who desires to learn more of the dark past of Ohio, this book will help you dive deeper into the hauntings of Licking County.

THE JOHNSTOWN WITCH

Concord Cemetery is a small resting place located on the east side of Johnstown, Ohio. Residents from all over Licking County have loved ones buried there, with some of its oldest graves dating back to the mid-1800s. The land that makes up Johnstown was originally given to a Revolutionary War veteran named John Alston Brown. Brown decided that he did not want to live in this area, so he sold his prize to Dr. Oliver Bigelow and relocated himself to Kentucky. Bigelow took to work to create and found the current sitting city in 1813.

As time passed, the town's population grew, and the original cemetery, the Bigelow Cemetery, could not hold all the deceased members of the community. The local church decided to buy property off businessman Isaac Miller with the intent of building a cemetery that the church could use for families that were in a financial struggle. The oldest section of the cemetery mostly consists of graves that are unmarked due to the lack of funds to get a proper headstone or because no family members were around to claim and bury the body elsewhere. Naturally, an old cemetery will have some urban legends to go along with it.

If you ask the Johnstown locals about Concord Cemetery, they will most likely tell you to visit on Halloween night. After midnight, if you approach the grave of Sarah Lovina, you might witness a green mist rising from the ground; if you're really lucky, you will see the spirit of a young girl roaming the area around that grave. Teenagers for decades have been sneaking into the cemetery after hours on Halloween to prove the story to be either true

The famous grave of Sarah Lovina, the Johnstown Witch.

or false to their friends. Why would the mist be coming out of this grave? Because Sarah Lovina is known as the Johnstown Witch.

Sarah was a thirteen-year-old girl back in the mid-1840s. She was witnessed having manic episodes and speaking in tongues and reportedly saw the shadow figure of a man with a large hat in her room, which was rumored to be the devil coming to trade her soul in exchange for mystical abilities. Some of the townsfolk accused Sarah of selling her soul for magic powers and becoming a witch. In an attempt to protect the town from her unholy reckoning, the city burned Sarah Lovina at the stake for the crime of witchcraft. Although this legend is interesting to share while trying to spook your friends around a campfire, the story is nothing more than a local urban legend.

The real story might not include the devil and magic powers, but some will argue that the truth is more fascinating. Sarah's last name was actually Emerson. Her last name was changed on her gravestone for reasons that remain unknown. Also, despite being buried in the same cemetery as her parents, she is not buried anywhere near them or anyone else in her family.

The true nature of Sarah's death is the result of a house fire, but no one knows exactly what caused the fire. Some reports say that Sarah knocked over an oil lamp on accident, while neighbors of the home reported seeing a person enter the house; they believed the fire to be the result of this home intruder. Fans of the urban legend share a story that Sarah had intentionally lit the house on fire to rid herself of the shadow man. One night, as the tale goes, as Sarah rested in bed trying to fall asleep, her bedroom door creaked open. Sarah looked into the hall to see a tall shadow with a large hat standing in her door frame. As the shadow man slowly approached the side of her bed, whispering empty promises of immortality and unstoppable power, Sarah jumped out of bed. Manic with fear, Sarah grabbed the oil lamp next to her bed and threw it at the shadow man. The lamp passed right through him as he disappeared. As the lamp hit the wall on the other side of the room, the curtains on her bedroom window lit up in flames. Sarah stared into the glow of the fire as an idea formed in her head. Determined to get rid of the shadow man for good, Sarah went through the house and lit every oil lamp she could find before smashing them on the floor. With the house consumed in flames, Sarah sat in the living room and waited for her nightmare to be over. The story of Sarah burning herself alive in a frenzy to stop the shadow man comes entirely from speculation, although there is no evidence that can *disprove* the story.

Over the years, Sarah's grave has become more and more popular. The church that sits on the land has burned down not once but twice for unexplainable reasons, and of course, Sarah's ghost is the speculated cause. The original church burned down soon after Sarah was first buried in the cemetery. After reconstruction, the church burned down a second time. After that, the city and organizations that look after the grounds decided to not rebuild the church. The legend surrounding Sarah is that if you visit her grave and tell her that you believe she was wrongfully accused and didn't deserve the hate from the town, then Sarah will grant you a wish or give you something that you are hoping for. However, if you tell Sarah that she was an evil witch who deserved to die, then something bad will happen in the town. A church will burn down or a citywide power outage will occur. It isn't uncommon to walk through the cemetery and notice people standing at Sarah's grave, talking to it while trying to test this legend. Local witch covens have also begun to include Sarah in their coven's lineage, going as far as to leave offerings and gifts on her grave. Locals have mentioned that they always seem to find coins, jewelry, toys, flowers, cakes, lighters or clothes at her resting place.

Visitors and members of the local witch coven leave coins on Sarah's grave as an offering.

Modern-day witches are very different from what people think. Most witches you encounter will describe themselves as practicing Wiccans, or non-denominational spiritual practitioners. These types of witches believe in a moral code nicknamed the Rule of 3, meaning that any energy that they direct at someone will come back to them threefold. If they send out positive energy or acts of magic, then positive energy will come back to them in their mind, body and spirit. If the witch decides to do harmful or negative acts with their practice, then they will receive negative energy back affecting every part of their lives. Some traditional Wiccans believe that negative energy coming back to them can affect everything in their life, including their health and appearance. Negative energy coming back to the mind will cause them to have severe depression, anxiety and mood swings, as well as forgetfulness and a lack of creativity. Negative energy coming back to their body can cause wrinkles, acne, sickness, aches and pains and loss of hair. This energy coming back to a witch's spirit can result in bad sleep, spells not working or going horribly wrong, lack of motivation to do anything with their day and a defeated feeling that they can't shake. This is why nearly every witch lives by the code "If it harms none, do as ye will," meaning that witches can practice their magic freely and as long as it doesn't hurt or negatively alter the life of anyone else, then the witches will not receive bad consequences. This is where the trope of ugly evil witches comes from. In most movies, if a witch is evil and greedy and attacks innocent people, then she is depicted as an ugly old lady with bad skin, horrible hair, missing teeth and a sour attitude. If there is a coven of witches in Johnstown, they probably aren't anything to worry about.

If the legends of witchcraft, deals with the devil and unexplainable arson don't give you the creeps already, Sarah's grave becomes even more eerie when you notice the poem written on her headstone. One would wonder why the family would leave such words on the grave of their daughter who was accused of being a witch. Through the erosion of the old stone, the poem reads as follows:

Young People all as you pass by
As you are now once was I
As I am now you soon will be
Prepare for death and follow me
My dust is mouldering back to dust
My soul returned to God
May those who read know soon they must
Lie cold beneath the clod.

Of Monster death why blast so soon
The flower that just began to bloom
But boast thou now weel not complain
For Sarah soon shall rise again
Then in that resurrection morn
We all shall meet her in the sky
From our cold graves dark and forlorn
We'll bask in scenes that never die.

People have noticed that the poem sounds more like a curse. It seems to be saying that children will die young, as she once did, and that Sarah will rise from the grave, never to die again. These Gothic words could be the source of the alleged green mist that rises on Halloween night, or maybe what people say is real and the mist is just the spirit of Sarah Emerson, rising from the grave to walk the earth again. This leaves people to wonder if maybe Sarah really did deal with the devil himself and now in death she holds a wicked power that can be used to do his work.

The most interesting part of the real-life events seems to be all the questions that remain. Why was Sarah's name changed on her headstone? Could it be that the family feared vandalism as a result of the rumors about her? Why would her parents choose to be buried so far away from her? Perhaps the family chose to change the name on Sarah's grave and bury themselves at a distance in order to remove themselves from the legend that surrounds her. What caused the fire that took Sarah's life, and what could be the cause of the fires that burned down the cemetery's church soon after Sarah's arrival?

As many people know from our history, the witch trials that swept through England and the rest of the United States were all nothing more than mass hysteria or a greedy attempt to take land and resources from other people in the community. If witchcraft and demonic activity are not the cause of Sarah's behavior and the unexplainable fires, then what could have caused them? We might never obtain the answers we need to eventually know the full story of Sarah's tragedy.

If you ever find yourself in Johnstown and need something to do, go visit Concord Cemetery and find this famous grave. Read the poem for yourself. Notice if you feel any strange energy in the air or if you witness any mist rising from the ground. Come up with your own theories as to what happened to the cemetery's church or what was causing Sarah's wicked behavior. And lastly, but most importantly, don't forget to leave a little gift for Sarah. Who knows if you have a coven of witches watching you to make sure you are being respectful.

LICKING COUNTY HISTORIC JAIL

Newark, Ohio, is home to many paranormal hot spots, but the most notable, as well as the most breathtaking, would be the Licking County Historic Jail. The jail was constructed in 1889 using stone from Millersburg, Ohio. It was unique at the time for two reasons. Firstly, it was crafted in the beautiful Richardson Romanesque style by Joseph Warren Yost, an architect from Columbus, Ohio. Yost worked for many years constructing county courthouses throughout Ohio, as well as Orton Hall at The Ohio State University. As president of the Western Division of Architects and partner of the architectural firm known as Yost & Packard, he had a great deal of notoriety among the population of Ohio and within the architectural society nationwide. The second reason the Licking County Historic Jail was so unique was due to how beautifully Gothic it was constructed. Yost crafted cat-like creatures into the windowsills, arched windows, turrets and towers. The design was so wonderful that even in modern times, it stands as one of the most toured locations in Central Ohio.

After construction in 1889, the jail began operation. Like many other jails of the time, the front three floors were used to house the current sitting sheriff and his family. The back of the building was where the inmates were housed and the functions of the jail happened. It originally held sixty-eight inmates, mostly men, with a separate floor for women, but by the 1970s, the county had moved the female inmates elsewhere to make room for more male inmates. Once the women were gone, the jail began to see more and more overcrowding. It became so difficult to run the facility smoothly that the jail was also struggling to maintain proper staff. The state soon updated the standards regarding how inmates of county jails should be treated and how a facility should operate. The Licking County Jail began failing every government standard.

Housing too many inmates led to the expected problems. The facility was more difficult to clean and sanitize, which in turn caused people to get sick. Disease would spread like wildfire due to the close quarters of the inmates. It was also becoming more and more difficult to run the facility safely because the inmates were growing agitated with the inhumane conditions and continuously rebelled against the authority. By 1987, a new larger facility had been completed, and the Licking County Historic Jail was closed. It was only in 2012 that the building was reopened for tours and community events with the help of the Licking County Governmental Preservation Society.

The jail was in operation for just under one hundred years, and in that time, it saw its share of murder, suicide and tragedy. Three sheriffs living on the grounds died in the living quarters from heart attacks. A fourth sheriff suffered a heart attack while in the home and died after being brought into the hospital. The building was later renovated to where the current sitting sheriff would no longer be living in the facility. The bedrooms were turned into offices and the living areas converted into conference rooms. In addition to the sheriffs, at least sixteen inmates died within the walls of the building. Eight of them had been the result of a suicide, and the rest, including some unsolved cases, were from murders or foul play.

Death was almost to be expected in a place like this just based on who was housed at this facility. Some of the most famous murderers of the time were sentenced here, sometimes together. For instance, murderess Laura Devlin was held in this jail before she was committed to Lima State Hospital and declared insane. The seventy-two-year-old woman murdered her husband after forty years of marriage. Her local postman had noticed that her husband had been missing for a few days. When he asked Laura about it, she showed him a postcard, allegedly from her husband's family in Philadelphia, explaining that he had died while visiting them and was soon to be buried. The postman noticed that there was no stamp on the card and grew suspicious. He led Laura to the police station to explain herself.

Laura was very cooperative with the police and calmly explained her story of what had actually happened to her husband. She informed them that her husband had threatened to kill her multiple times throughout their marriage and was physically abusive for most of their relationship. One day, while in an argument, he began to throw dishes at her. Something in her snapped, and her instincts instructed her to fight back. After beating him to death with her bare hands, she used a handsaw to remove his head, arms and legs. She then attempted to burn them in her oven to dispose of any evidence and hid his torso in her backyard. The police arrested Laura immediately. Ever since her trial, she has been known as the "Handsaw Slayer."

Laura was not the only gruesome murderer housed in Licking County Jail. The jail also housed Louis Angel and Harmon Cordray, two U.S. marines who went AWOL; they were also known as the "Route 40 Hitchhike Slayers." The two men had abandoned the base where they were stationed and were hitchhiking west when they murdered a taxi driver for seemingly unknown reasons. The "San Quentin Parole Murderer," Harold Shackleford, was sentenced here too, along with many other locally infamous killers. Most of them were given life sentences and spent their final days behind the bars of this facility. But have their spirits ever left?

Most fans of the ghost hunting show *Ghost Adventures* might recognize the name of this jail. In season 12 of the show, which aired in 2014, paranormal celebrity Zak Bagans and his team of investigators were invited to Newark to investigate the jail. In 2017, another paranormal celebrity, Chad Lindberg, also visited the jail to investigate. Both investigation teams captured disembodied voices and objects being moved, and Chad's team even caught the ghostly apparition of Mayor Herbert Atherton in a photo. You can find this photo displayed on the Licking County Historic Jail's website.

In addition to the television stars who investigated the jail, it has also attracted the attention of internet paranormal celebrities. Social media has given a platform to average people to voice their thoughts and interests, which can gain them an online following of likeminded people. YouTube lets people post self-made videos that can be shared among their followers and be suggested to new viewers who are watching similar videos. Hauntings and paranormal investigation videos have been on the rise in the past decade. One of the most popular paranormal internet celebrities is Elton Castee.

Elton and his group of friends filmed the most viewed internet video of the Licking County Historic Jail in July of 2021, garnering more than 1 million views. In that video, the team heard unexplainable noises and witnessed motion sensor lights being set off without an explainable cause, flashlights flickering and turning on by themselves without being touched and doors closing by themselves. They also recorded spikes of energy on their EMF (electromagnetic field) readers and recorded video of toys and a ball being played with by unseen hands.

The Licking County Historic Jail has been investigated by dozens of paranormal teams over the years.

Through almost an entire century, this jail has seen death within its somber walls. Due to the negative nature of the environment, the fact that some very violent and evil people have taken their lives or passed away on the grounds and documented proof and testimony from some of the most famous ghost hunters in the country, you can imagine how this place has become a famous haunted tourist attraction. People can pay to attend private or public ghost investigations at the historic jail and spend the night trying to create proof of their own that there is more to life than what we experience before we die.

There is such a thing as an afterlife, and for some reason, some spirits spend theirs here on earth. People used to think the weather was caused by the gods, but we now know the natural circumstances that create it. As science advances, what we currently consider paranormal might one day be explained and described as normal. Maybe soon we will learn what circumstances cause people's spirits trapped here in our physical world. Or we may never know what caused the spirits of these people to remain in this facility or anywhere else that you can find ghosts. But you could be taking the opportunity to communicate with the ones that were left here and attempt to learn about things that no living person currently understands.

If you are curious about the paranormal and need a starting point to begin your research and investigation, look into Licking County's historic jail. There are almost two dozen known spirits in this building that are just dying to share their stories, so to speak.

The Legend of the Black Hand

The push for environmental protection has been around for a long time. Some of the most influential work toward the movement took place throughout the Unites States between the 1930s and the 1950s. The movement gained so much traction and the public opinion of conserving our environment became so strong that the Wilderness Act was signed into law in 1964 by President Lyndon Johnson. Land was being sectioned off to form natural parks and reserves to make sure that industrialization would not disturb wildlife in the area. Ohio has a handful of nature preservations, but one of the most famous is the Blackhand Gorge State Nature Preserve.

The sights in this preserve are one of a kind. Blackhand Gorge has the only bike trail in the entire nature preserve system in Ohio. The Licking River flows through the gorge, slowly eroding the earth to create a deeper stream. Sandstone lines the river for the area's wildlife to stand on while drinking from the water. Both sides of the gorge host cliffs that stand hundreds and hundreds of feet high. In addition to the beautiful natural scenery, people have also visited Blackhand Gorge for its history. In 1828, during the construction of the Ohio-Erie Canal, settlers used dynamite to blow off pieces of the cliff and helped shape it into what it is today. While walking on the trails, visitors can still see the towpath and locks from the old canal.

The gorge originally got its name from a large carving in the face of one of the cliffs that appeared to be a large black hand. The black hand is no longer on the face of the cliff, as it was blown off with the stone that was being cleared for the canal. It is believed that the reason for the carving was to serve as a reminder of an urban legend that was shared among the tribe that lived on the land before the canal's construction. Ever since the story was first discovered, the Legend of the Black Hand has been a popular ghost story to tell throughout this region of Ohio.

Blackhand Gorge has hours of hiking trails to explore.

A long time ago, a Native American tribe lived on the land that now makes up the nature preserve. The chief of this tribe was named Powkongah, and he was respected as not only an amazing leader but also a strong warrior and political diplomat. Powkongah had only one child, a daughter by the name of Ahyoma, who was the most beautiful woman in the tribe. Her skin was fair, her eyes were gentle and captivating and her voice was soft and enchanting. Ahyoma attracted the attention of two young men in her tribe: a pair of brothers known as Wacousta and Lahkopis. Both were in love with Ahyoma, and it was far from a secret. Everyone in the tribe was aware of their infatuation, including Ahyoma's father. What wasn't known, however, was that Ahyoma was also in love with Lahkopis, the younger brother of the pair.

One day, the chief approached the young warriors and gave them a challenge. The men were to head into battle with the rest of the armies defending their homeland. The brother who collected the most scalps after three months of combat would win the hand of Ahyoma in marriage. Wacousta eagerly joined the ranks. As the elder brother with more combat experience, he was confident that he would be the victor. On the other hand, although Lahkopis was more inexperienced, but he had a burning passion to step out his brother's shadow and claim Ahyoma as his wife.

After three months had passed, the brothers returned and stepped before Chief Powkongah at the top of the cliff where his home sat. The chief stood firmly, with his men around him, ready to claim a winner of his challenge. Unbeknownst to everyone, Ahyoma watched the scene from the safety of her lodge. First, Wacousta approached the chief. He presented his belt, which was full of dozens upon dozens of scalps. He received praise from the other men, while Ahyoma watched on in fear that her love, Lahkopis, had lost the challenge. As Lahkopis's stomach turned with anxiety, he set his belt down next to Wacousta's. The chief counted the scalps slowly and carefully before his eyes lit up in excitement. He threw his hands in the air, exclaiming that Wacousta's belt had one more scalp, and thus, he was the winner. As the crowd cheered, Powkongah retrieved his daughter and presented her before Wacousta so the two could meet formally.

As Wacousta took her hand into his and introduced himself, Ahyoma jerked her arm away and ran to Lahkopis. She confessed to her father that she was in love with Lahkopis and refused to marry Wacousta. Offended, Wacousta challenged Lahkopis to a contest of his own: a fight to the death, with the winner getting to claim Ahyoma for their own. Lahkopis accepted, and both men drew their tomahawks to begin the duel. As the brother's battled, Lahkopis managed to sever Wacousta's right hand at the wrist, watching both the hand and the tomahawk fall to the ground. Lahkopis exclaimed that he did not want to kill his brother and asked Wacousta to admit defeat before it resulted in his death.

Powkongah claimed Lahkopis as the winner of the battle, and Ahyoma ran into the arms of her lover. As the two embraced, Wacousta let out a howl of anger and charged at his brother. He managed to tackle not only Lahkopis but Ahyoma as well, and the three of them fell off the edge of the cliff to their deaths in the river below. The only remains to be found of the love triangle was Wacousta's severed hand, which sat in the grass on top of the cliff. As a reminder of the tragedy that had taken place in the village, the hand was left at the top of the cliff overlooking the river below. As time passed, the hand grew black with rot. Once the hand became unrecognizable, the chief decided to carve the image of a large black hand into the face of the cliff so the story of the death of his daughter would be remembered. Never again should the power of love be overlooked. The carving remained for generations until it was blasted off with dynamite by the canal builders.

Today, the legend of the black hand has been shared so much that everyone seems to hear a different version. Some say that Ahyoma and Lahkopis ran away together after Lahkopis had collected more scalps and that Wacousta cut off his own hand in scorn to curse his brother. The reason that first version of the story is told more often is because the spirits of Ahyoma and Lahkopis are frequently spotted throughout Blackhand Gorge. Over the years, people have reported seeing and hearing a Native American woman kneeling over and sobbing at top of the cliff. She can be seen peeking out from around the trees in the nature preserve, watching visitors hike the trails. Once someone notices her, she will disappear without a trace. People have heard native drums in the woods. Witnesses have investigated the area to find the source of the drumming sound—perhaps an oil drum in the area is causing the noise, but oil drums do not exist on a nature preserve. Explorers have also reported the faint sound of combat on top of the cliff, as if Lahkopis and Wacousta have never ended their battle over Ahyoma. Paranormal teams have visited the area to investigate the sightings of the lover spirits. The most popular piece of evidence are EVPs (electronic voice phenomena) of a disembodied male voice speaking into a voice recorder. Investigators have tried to debunk the EVPs because of how easily the wind blows through the nature preserve, but the voice is too commonly captured and too clearly understood for some to believe it comes from natural causes.

The Blackhand Gorge has jaw-dropping scenery and interesting American history to cherish, so it is highly recommended that all Ohioans visit at some point. If you ever make the trip, be sure to tell the story of how the gorge got its name with your travel companions and share with them the legend of Ahyoma and the feuding brothers. See if you can witness any ghostly happenings, and feel free to use the story to give your friends the creeps. Head to the top of the cliff and overlook the breathtaking view of the land around you. But please, be careful—according to the legend, you won't survive a fall.

Cedar Hill Cemetery

Cedar Hill Cemetery is located on North Cedar Street in Newark. Unlike most cemeteries or paranormal hot spots, this creepy graveyard doesn't have just *one* urban legend associated with it. The residents of the area can share hours' worth of folklore and personal stories of the happenings of this cemetery. The first burial happened in 1850, and the land holds the bodies of soldiers from every conflict that our country has taken part in since World War I. This cemetery is the largest in Licking County, and some of its most prominent residents are buried here.

One family is famous due to the spooky nature of the crypt. The Baker family crypt, just off from the center of the cemetery, has a large rustic door guarded by the statue of an angel. The iron fence surrounding the crypt adds a beautiful touch. The Gothic stylings have earned this crypt the nickname "the Asylum." Local legend says that if you approach the big metal door of the Asylum, knock three times and put your ear up against it, you will hear muffled voices and horrible screaming. Some believe this legend, but most who know of the legend have attempted to knock on the door themselves and report that nothing happened. Although this sounds like a ritual that someone would practice late at night with a full moon out, the Cedar Hill Cemetery locks its gates at 8:00 p.m., so it's unclear when the best time to complete this challenge really is. Maybe the lack of moonlight is what's causing all the skepticism.

It looks as though six members of the Baker family were entombed in the Asylum, with most of their deaths occurring in the late 1800s. Theories have circulated about whether the Baker family were haunted, which would

Cedar Hill Cemetery is one of the largest burial grounds in Ohio.

cause the strange activity. People have also theorized that they were a group of serial killers and that the screaming voices belong to their victims. However, there are no news articles or police reports documenting anything supernatural or criminal related to the Bakers resting inside the Asylum. It is safe to say that the legend is only shared for fun and that the Baker crypt should be visited respectfully.

Another popular urban legend of the cemetery is the Baby Face Statue. Just left of the Asylum, almost directly in the center of Cedar Hill, stands that statue of a baby's face, carved into the headstone of Jane Malloby. Jane was originally married to a man named Wilfred Smith. After Smith's death, Jane stayed close to his family until the new widow met Reverend Thomas Malloby. The two married and lived out the rest of Jane's life together. After Jane passed away, the Malloby and Smith families invested in her burial. The large tombstone with the baby statue featured on the front honors her memory and adds an innocent touch to her grave.

The Baby Face Statue has gathered more popularity than any other monument in the cemetery. People report that if you stare into the baby's face for a few minutes, look away and then return your gaze back to the baby, the baby's eyes will be looking in a different direction. Unlike the Baker family crypt, this urban legend has a much larger population of believers. Photos and videos have been taken to "prove" that the baby statue has a mind of its own and the capability to watch its visitors. Skeptics of the legend have chalked it up to an optical illusion based on the change of the sunlight that strikes the stone.

Top: The Baker family crypt, known as the Asylum.

Left: Jane Malloby's famous headstone.

Above: Legend says that if you state into the baby's face for a few minutes, look away and then look again, its eyes will be looking in another direction.

Another incredibly famous grave in this cemetery belongs to the resting place of John Veach, who was present during the assassination of President Abraham Lincoln. An old legend told throughout the historical societies of Newark talks about how Newark's own John Veach worked as a pass inspector on the night of the assassination. Veach was checking military passes at the doors of Ford's Theatre before earning the ability to go attend the show. He recounted that he was sitting in the back of the theater in the company of Major White when they heard the gunshot.

Veach and the major ran to the box to assist the president when he saw John Wilkes Booth jump from the box rail to the stage below. Booth had caught his left foot in the flag that was hanging on the box rail and injured himself in his fall. Veach and the major were the first people at the scene of the crime, and they decided that they needed to get the president to safety. The men grabbed the president and took him across the street to a private residence in an attempt to give the doctors time to save him. Unfortunately, they failed, and Lincoln died.

An article published in the *Newark Advocate* in 2011 titled "Who Held Lincoln's Head" pointed out that a lot of the legend has too many plot holes to be true. It was Dr. Charles Leale who was first on the scene, as he was seated fairly close by at the time of the president's assassination. Official reports and a number of eyewitnesses reported that Laura Keene was actually holding the president's head in her lap while Leale and other doctors worked to save him. The doctors and some other witnesses had been the ones to carry Lincoln out of the theater. Veach is not mentioned in any of the official statements about the events.

Actually, the main source of this story originated straight from John Veach himself. He was telling his tale of saving the president at the age of seventy-five at the pension office, and he seemed to be getting some of his information wrong. Major White was in command over the company to which Veach belonged, but he had been promoted to a general just before the events of the theater had taken place. Anyone who served in the infantry would be sure to call a commanding officer by his proper rank, and if Veach was working under White throughout his service as well as on the night of the assassination, wouldn't he be aware of the change in title?

The plot holes could also be explained. As mentioned before, John Veach was recounting the events as an old man. There is a chance that he simply reverted to referring to White as a major out of habit. Veach very well also could have been one of the unnamed bystanders who helped carry Lincoln out of the theater, but he most certainly wasn't first on the scene. The only detail that is confirmed to be absolutely true is that Veach was at Ford's Theatre on the night of the assassination, and he was seated in a section that would allow him to reach Lincoln's box in a reasonable amount of time.

This story that Veach shared was passed around town for generations. This could be what inspired the final urban legend of Cedar Hill Cemetery. People report that when you take pictures of Veach's grave, the images capture a large bright orb of light near the headstone. Paranormal fans believe that the orb is the spirit of Veach standing guard over himself and the other Civil War veterans buried at the cemetery. People have also heard a disembodied male voice yelling for help in the section where Veach's grave is located. When witnesses rush to the area, they find no one there. It is rumored that the voice is actually Veach calling for the doctors to come help him save the president.

Sitting on 133 acres of land, Cedar Hill Cemetery has a lot of ground to explore. At this point, it is almost a rite of passage for anyone who resides in the area to take their friends to the graveyard and challenge them to knock on the Asylum and stare at the Baby Face Statue. If you are a skeptic, try it yourself and prove your point! Just remember that the legends must have started somewhere. Be prepared for anything that might happen.

THE BUXTON INN

In addition to the cities that hold most of the population of Licking County, there's also a series of towns small enough to be considered villages. One of these is Granville, and despite being small, the village is rich with history. It holds a lot of historical buildings, like St. Luke's Episcopal Church and the Avery Downer House. Granville also has one of the oldest colleges in the area, Denison University. However, no building in this region of Ohio is nearly as famous as the Buxton Inn.

Granville has been around for a long time, and so has the Inn. The Buxton Inn's website states that migrating families from Massachusetts and Connecticut settled this part of Ohio back in 1805. The area got its name from an older settlement where the group once lived. The population grew as more families began building houses and starting to work in the area, and Granville was officially declared a village in 1832, which it has remained ever since. One of the first businesses to be established in the area was called "The Tavern," owned by Orrin Granger, in 1812. The Tavern became the village's first post office and allowed mail and goods to be transported from Granville to the larger cities in the area, which were Newark and Columbus. The Tavern had a large stagecoach stop for the drivers. Stagecoach drivers would cook themselves meals and utilize the dining room and soon were given the ability to rent spaces in the basement to sleep. The Tavern operated accordingly for many years, even while the building was being renovated and expanded as it changed owners after Granger's death. Finally, in 1865, The Tavern was bought by Major Horton Buxton. Since the space was popularly known as an area for travelers to come for food and a bed, Buxton converted The Tavern into a hotel and renamed the building the Buxton Inn. The Inn operated under Major Buxton and his family until 1934, when Bonnie Bounell took over due to the major's death.

The Buxton Inn is among the oldest standing businesses in Granville, Ohio.

Bonnie lived in one of the rooms of the Inn with her cat, named after Major Buxton, until she passed away in room 9 in 1960; a man who had helped her operate the Buxton Inn, Nell Schoeller, became the new owner. Nell held possession of the Inn for a short while before he sold it to Orrville Orr and his wife, Audrey, in 1972. Orrville and Audrey revolutionized the business. They restored and renovated the building to be a much cozier space. The couple held ownership of the Inn until they sold the property to the preservation society and retired.

The Buxton Inn has sat on the same plot of land since the building was originally constructed back in the early years of the village's founding. Nowadays, people visit the Inn for many different reasons. Some are looking for a cozy place to stay. Some want to experience the history of the town. Some people come to explore the hidden passages and stairways that hid the escaping slaves during the Underground Railroad, and others want to have a drink in the location that was once used to operate a speakeasy during Prohibition. But most of all, visitors come to investigate the reported hauntings!

Both the employees and the nightly visitors over the years have reported a mind-blowing amount of paranormal activity at the Buxton Inn. The majority of people who step foot into the building report the unshakable feeling that someone or something is watching their every move. Guests have also reported hearing and sometimes seeing the shadow of footsteps under the door, just outside of their rooms, in the dead of night. These footsteps are not just passing through the halls, but they appear to be pacing in front of certain rooms and will sometimes stop and stand at the door for prolonged periods of time. Some guests have decided to get out of bed to investigate the stranger standing outside their room, only to open the door and find nobody there. A former employee of the Buxton Inn named John Englehardt began working at the Inn in 1978, when he was

Former presidents, artists, musicians and actors all throughout history have visited the Buxton Inn. It was also used as a stop on the Underground Railroad.

still a high schooler. Englehardt has said many times that he believed the building to be haunted without a doubt.

Englehardt reported that he had a ghostly experience during a night shift within his first year of employment. He said that he was working alone and had already locked the place up and began doing his nighttime duties. While in the basement, he began hearing footsteps on the floor above him. No one should have access those rooms, so he headed upstairs and began checking the locks to make sure no one had gotten in. Once he had found that the locks were still intact, he searched the floor to find anyone or anything that could have made the noise. The next day, he asked Mr. Orr if he had returned to the Inn for any reason the night before, and Mr. Orr told Englehardt that he hadn't. With no possible explanation, John believed that the source of the footsteps was from the spirit of either a past resident or a former owner of the Inn.

Englehardt couples this story with another that he remembers from his time working at the Inn. He was working a shift one day and had just returned from a break when he was approached by the head chef of the kitchen. The head chef was panicked and exasperated, telling him that while he was napping in room 9 on his break, a lady wearing all blue had pushed him out of the bed and onto the floor before disappearing into thin air. The Lady in Blue has become a very common sighting at the Buxton Inn. Audrey

Orr remembered a busy night in the 1990s. A nurse who was staying in room 9 reported to management that she was visited by a woman wearing a blue gown the previous night. The woman entered her room and had a conversation with her before leaving. The nurse was wondering who could possibly have had access to her room besides the staff, and she wanted to know who the woman was. The staff had informed the nurse of the Inn's haunted history and let her know that a previous owner, Bonnie Bounell, had lived and died in room 9. In life, she was known for wearing a lot of blue and checking on the guests for quality customer service.

The spirit of Bonnie is in company with the spirit of her cat, Major Buxton. In addition to those spirits, guests and employees have also reported seeing the spirit of the original Inn's owner, Major Buxton himself, and his wife. It is believed that Orrin Granger is also roaming the Inn's walls at night, admiring what his tavern was turned into. Many of these spirits are seen as orbs or sometimes as clear apparitions in photographs. Many guests within the past few decades have had most of their sightings of the Lady in Blue occur while they were taking pictures in the mirror. Bonnie tends to be seen in the mirror behind them.

In addition to room 9, room 7 is also reported to be a hot spot for paranormal activity. Full-body shadow figures have been sighted in this room, as well as disembodied voices calling out names in the hallway. Guests who stay in room 7 have also heard the strange sound of change being spilled over the floor, and they can never seem to find the source of what caused the sound. There have also been reports of a random old-fashioned floral scent that comes and goes throughout room 7 with an unexplainable cause. In the basement of the Buxton Inn, many employees over the years have reported shadow figures and sometimes will see the spirit of a young boy peering out around shelves. Who this young boy is remains unknown.

Any true paranormal investigator of Ohio absolutely must investigate the Buxton Inn in Granville at some point in his or her career. If you want to learn more about the hauntings and paranormal discoveries that have been found over the years, the Inn has made an appearance on most paranormal podcasts, TV shows and haunting-related YouTube channels. Single- and double-person rooms can be booked based on availability on the Buxton Inn's website. Go explore the old walls of the building and discover the secret doors and passages that were used during the Underground Railroad. Stay in a room that was once inhabited by famous guests, such as Abraham Lincoln, President William Henry Harrison and author Harriet Beecher Stowe.

Make sure you ask some employees about any personal paranormal experiences they might have from working at the old hotel. If you find any evidence of an intelligent haunting during your stay, be sure to share it online! The history of these types of buildings can be better preserved with the funding that their community and their fans provide when they visit. The Buxton Inn is one of the most popular paranormal locations in all of Ohio, so if you have never seen a ghost before, that is a great place to start.

THE CAPTAIN'S GHOST

Have you ever seen a ghost? How do you think you would react if you did? Some people are fascinated by their ghostly encounters because they see it as proof that our spirit can live on after our body's death. Most paranormal fans or new investigators get started because they had an unexpected encounter with the paranormal that fascinated them enough to begin investigating for answers of the afterlife. It sometimes brings a reassuring feeling that we do not just disappear to be forgotten forever once our mortal time on this planet is up. However, most people have the opposite reaction. They are so shocked and terrified of their paranormal experience that they freeze up or run away. After seeing a ghost, some people will never return to the location of the sighting as long as they live. One popular legend from Newark is about how a series of paranormal encounters were so scary that the establishment where they occurred had to be closed. That would be the legend of the Captain's Ghost.

The initial construction of the Ohio & Erie Canal began at Licking Summit on July 4, 1825. The canal ran through downtown Newark, exactly where what is now known as Canal Street sits. The canal was put here to make it easier to bring goods and products to the businesses in the town that were helping the population and economy grow. The addition of the canal was an incredibly important part of the rise of business and population of early Newark. The people arriving on the tugboats would either be heading to Newark to buy property and begin a new life, or they were just passing through the city to get to another destination. Unfortunately for some, the soil of the county's seat would be the last that they would step foot on.

The captains and crew of the tugboats didn't stay in one place for very long. They were usually working, so they would spend most of their time on the boats traveling from city to city. That meant that most of them didn't own property or have families because they wouldn't be home very often, if at all. It became common that a city would build a tavern and a hotel of some sort in addition to their canals so that the crew of the tugboats would have a place to relax and sleep before setting off on another trip. Newark was no exception. The south side of Newark's square, nicknamed Gingerbread Row, held most of the temporary housing where the canal crews would stay. Gingerbread Row was full of inns, bars, restaurants and gaming or gambling halls.

One night, a tugboat captain was enjoying his evening by having drinks with his crewmates at the tavern. Late into the night, the captain decided it was time to retire to his room at the inn so he could get his rest and set off to Akron the next day. The captain began walking back to the inn, all alone, but for some odd reason, he couldn't shake a dark and eerie presence in the air. Thinking nothing of it, he entered the inn and approached the door of his room when he paused. Faintly, he could hear footsteps and the sound of rifling through drawers from inside his room. The captain pulled out his hunting knife and reached for the handle of the door. He twisted the handle slowly and quietly before quickly jerking the door open and rushing inside with his knife held above his head. As soon as he lunged through the door, he was stopped dead in his tracks seeing a loaded pistol pointed directly at his face. A large burglar was standing in his room in front of an open window that faced the street. Threatening the captain's life, the burglar demanded that the captain hand over his money and valuables. The captain, fearing for his life, handed over his hunting knife, pocket watch and all the money he was carrying on him. Once the captain was checked to make sure he wasn't hiding anything else on his person, he was forced at gunpoint to go through the room and collect the valuables he had in his belongings. Once the burglar pocketed everything worth stealing from the room, he executed the captain with a bullet to the back of his head. The burglar then carried the captain's body out of the window of the inn, tossed him into the canal and ran into the night. The body of the captain lay in the canal all night. The next day, as the crew was getting itself together to set off for its next destination, the men discovered their captain floating in the water. With no evidence left behind at the scene besides the ransacked bedroom, the murder went unsolved.

Rumors and theories about the murder at the inn spread throughout the community. Fear was established among the masses that the killer was not found, and there was no evidence left behind that provided any hope of authorities finding him. People were too afraid to rent a room in that inn after the murder because everyone believed that the rooms lacked security. It was the talk of the town to not rent a room at the southside inn because murderers and robbers were hanging around in dark alleys waiting to take advantage of visitors. Lock workers would even warn the captains and crew of future tugboats to avoid the inn, or it would cost them their lives. The owner of the inn renovated the building to increase security measures of the business and the rooms to help put people's fear at ease. Slowly, people began returning to the inn, only to discover a new reason to be terrified of the establishment.

Sightings of the ghost of the captain breathed new life into the infamy of the rooming house. Guests on the second floor of the inn would report waking up in the middle of the night to find the captain standing at the end of their bed. People on the ground level reported hearing footsteps above them on the second floor of the building late at night, even though employees reassured them that no one was up there. Employees of the establishment would even quit their jobs out of fear and share stories with their friends and community about the haunting they endured while at work. Those working at the inn would put out candles in the office and other areas that only employees should be in before leaving for the night, only to return in the morning to find them relit. They would have documents go missing and feel unseen hands grab their arms or shoulders. One former employee reported that he took a nap in a spare room after a night shift only to be woken up from a choking sensation on his neck. It felt as though someone had wrapped their hands around his throat and were trying to choke him to death in his sleep!

It was becoming harder and harder to keep staff at the establishment. It was rumored that the captain's ghost would not be able to be at peace until his murderer was brought to justice. Between the unsolved murder and the growing number of ghost stories, the inn lost all of its business and closed down. The property has changed owners and businesses time and time again over the last 150 years, where it is now the H&R Block on South Park Place.

You might notice that the story is missing some details, such as who the killer was, the name of the captain or the official name of the rooming house where the events took place. Some people say that the names and other important details are scarce due to the nature of the murder. No evidence was left behind and the murder went unsolved, so the identity of the killer will never be known. Also, tugboat crews lived nomadic lives. It didn't make much sense for them to have a house and a family if they would be living on a boat and traveling all over Ohio during an era when traveling was very time-consuming. The captain wouldn't have had many things affiliated with his name, and his crew most likely called him by his rank. He was also only in the town for one night before being murdered, so it is unlikely that his name would be known by anyone who lived in Newark. The name of the inn was also changed before going out of business, and then it continually changed with the new ownership over time. The business owners most likely did whatever they could to let some of the details of the event subside in order to distance themselves from the negative publicity. People have also speculated that the story isn't true and was just an old tale that the locals and crews would share while drunk at the taverns to freak one another out.

The story seemed to work, though, because the tale of the Captain's Ghost is one of the most popular urban legends in the state. You can hear the story on any of the city's ghost tours, haunted webpages and forums, and it's told around a fire during Halloween or summer camp. Share the story with your friends to try and give them a scare or use it as a friendly reminder to always lock up before heading out for a night on the town. You never know who or what you'll find in your house when you return if you don't.

DENISON UNIVERSITY

The Buxton Inn might be the most well-known haunted location in Granville, but it is not the most trafficked. In fact, most people don't even realize when they are standing on the most haunted property in all of Granville. For the past 190 years, the majority of the student and faculty population of Denison University have been blissfully unaware of the paranormal happenings of the campus. However, for some, the university was one of the most active and terrifying haunting sites in the state. If you are an applicant considering further study at the college, a current student at the school or an alumnus who has graduated some time since the university was founded in 1831, you might want to take a look into its haunted history!

Denison University has been standing for almost 200 years. For a country that is only 245 years old to date, that is an accomplishment that the citizens of Granville and the graduates of the university should take great pride in. The campus is beautifully constructed, with every building made of clean stone or bright-red brick. According to the university's website, Denison held its first classes while Andrew Jackson was the nation's president. The university's founders were attempting to create an educational space to create the type of citizens who would lead the new country to greatness, so they turned to graduates of Brown University in Rhode Island to guide them in establishing what was then known as the Granville Literary and Theological Institution. As the college grew, obtained more funding and popularity, and established a more diverse curriculum, the institution was renamed to Granville College before eventually being rebranded as Denison University in the mid-1850s.

Denison University is believed to be the most haunted college campus in the state.

People from all over the nation attended the new university, meaning that people from a variety of backgrounds gathered in a shared space. Being exposed to so many different groups of people and cultures had led to swinging the political climate for many people of the university to be more liberal in thinking. Denison's early students were very active in vocalizing their support for the abolition of slavery and to grant equal rights to women. Students and alumni would actively protest, sometimes on campus and sometimes at government buildings. Their activism resulted in the construction of women's colleges in Granville. Soon after that, the new women's college was integrated into Denison so women were able to join the classes with the men. Today, the university has expanded into a massive institution for further learning, welcoming all students from all walks of life.

The major component that makes this university so unique isn't its rich history or impressive history of activism, but the fact that the university has a cemetery on campus. Once the college began to expand in its early development, the university took ownership of the hill where the already established cemetery was sitting. Rather than tearing up the cemetery, the university decided to expand right over it. The cemetery still has some of its original inhabitants of the early settlers of Granville, but some of the bodies were moved in order to make space. Ever since acquiring the cemetery, most of the new burials have been Denison faculty and graduates who accomplished great things during their lives. Many of the university's past presidents and their families are buried here as well. Having a university that is almost as old as our country that hosts a cemetery filled with influential people of its history is the perfect recipe for a haunting.

Denison University has enough ghost stories and paranormal activity to scare the pants off the new freshman class each year. The campus library is the most well-known haunted location of the school. The spirit of a lady in an old-fashioned dress has been reported throughout the library, but her home seems to be the seventh floor. She has a strict, no-nonsense type of personality and seems to be particularly displeased with male students. A large number of men attending the university have reported falling asleep on the seventh floor of the library while studying, only to be slapped over the back of the head and woken up by this ghostly woman, who immediately vanishes. She has also been seen peering out between bookshelves and watching the student's study. When the woman is spotted glaring at her victims through the shelves, she will disappear into thin air. Some students have decided to properly investigate the library in the past and have captured digital images of the woman, as well as recordings of a disembodied female voice and videos of books being knocked off of the shelves by themselves. It is suspected that the spirit of the woman is that of a wife of one of the early presidents, but no one has been able to confirm the theory. A popular social media app known as Yik Yak was common among most college campuses in the mid-2010s. A lot of paranormal reports would gain popularity on Yik Yak since it was a quick and entertaining way for students to share their experiences. One of the highest up-voted, or liked, posts on Yik Yak was from 2015, when a male student shared his personal experience in the library. He had posted that he was sitting in the library working on a research assignment when he felt as if someone was watching him. He glanced up to see an old woman standing in an aisle of books, staring at him with an angry snarl on her face. Confused, the student stared at this angry woman, thinking, "What is this old lady so mad about?" Another student, looking down at her phone and not noticing the woman in front of her, walked right *through* the old woman as she made her way down the aisle of books. Once the other student passed through the old woman, the woman vanished. This story remained as one of the top posts about the school until the app shut down in 2017.

In addition to the library, one of the dorm rooms on campus is also rumored to be haunted. Chamberlain Lodge has had reports of hauntings for the past six decades. Students residing on the second floor have reported inexplicably chilly temperatures that appear in spots throughout their rooms or come over the entire room before vanishing and returning the room back to normal. People have also reported having their belongings torn off the walls, knocked off dressers and desks or going missing all together. During the very early hours of the morning, residents have felt their blankets being slowly pulled off them in their sleep, felt the weight of a person sitting on the side of their bed when no one was there or felt unseen hands run through their hair. Some students think that living in the "haunted dorm" is cool and will treat the spirits like a friend or a pet. Other students are deeply worried about the situation and will request to switch rooms or abandon their dorm room to go live elsewhere.

The chapel on campus sees its fair share of paranormal activity too. Swasey Chapel has an urban legend of its own that has been shared for generations among the student body. The basement of the chapel is rumored to be home to a poltergeist. Candles that have been arranged in the basement have been said to light up suddenly, by themselves, in the shape of an upside-down cross when people approach it. Students who have unwisely decided to explore the chapel's basement have reported hearing footsteps throughout that level of the building when no one else is there to create them and being overcome with an overwhelming feeling of dread and fear. If you can last longer than twenty minutes in the basement without running and screaming for your life, then you are braver than most of the student body that has explored there in the past. However, it is strongly encouraged that no students enter the basement without proper approval. Do you think that is because the administration wants to keep things from being stolen or vandalized, or because they know that the poltergeist in the basement is dangerous?

Lastly, the cemetery mentioned earlier has its own ghost story or two. Students and faculty walking past the cemetery at night have seen the shadow figure of a young boy within the gates. This shadow boy seems to be very playful. He has been seen poking his head around tombstones like he is playing a game of hide-and-seek, or sometimes he is seen running through the cemetery and weaving through the graves. Rumors of the child shadow spirit have been spread since the late 1800s, and although reports are less frequent now, he still appears from time to time. Who might this spirit belong to? The most popular theory is that the boy's body was one of the early graves buried in the cemetery before the land was bought and occupied by the university.

If you are attending Denison University, don't be afraid. The alleged hauntings are just another fascinating detail that makes the campus so

Left: Denison University Chapel's basement is said to be haunted by a poltergeist.

Below: A cemetery was acquired as the university bought more land to expand on. Rather than remove the cemetery, the university just kept building right past it.

unique. You can use these stories to freak out your friends or any new students you meet in class. You could also use what you know of the hauntings to do some investigating of your own. The next time you need a break from studying for finals, go see if you can spot the ghost in the library. Just try not to fall asleep, or you might end up having one of the most confusing and scary awakenings of your life.

Bryn Du Mansion

Have you ever driven past a large, old, isolated property and immediately thought to yourself, "That place is definitely haunted"? Haunted mansions and plantations seem to be a common trope in the paranormal world, since these properties are famously known for being built by the family. Sometimes, these family members don't want to leave their property, even after death. And who can blame them? It's forever been the American dream to have a large house packed with a loving family that sits on acres upon acres of land. The home will be passed down through generations of the family before someone eventually loses the ability to keep up with the maintenance of the estate. Then the grand home will be sold to another family, and the process starts all over again. Granville, Ohio, has a famously haunted mansion of its own, and its beautifully constructed walls are full of secrets and stories just waiting to be explored.

The Bryn Du Mansion is currently owned by the Village of Granville and has a comprehensive telling of its history posted on its website, using information collected by the Granville Ohio Historical Society. The mansion was built by Henry D. Wright back in 1865 using sandstone gathered right off the property itself. The estate was sold to Jonas McCune and was promptly renamed McCune's Villa. Over the next forty years, ownership of the property changed hands a number of times. After striking it rich in the coal and railroad industries, John Sutphin Jones bought McCune's Villa in 1905. John Jones renamed the property to Bryn Du, which translates to Dark Hills in Welsh.

The entry gate to Bryn Du Mansion.

Jones renovated the mansion and constructed the outbuildings using the help of architect Frank Packard. The two men also built and established the Granville Inn together in June 1924, using land that once held the Granville Female College. The gymnasium building was renovated and connected to the Inn to create more guest bedrooms. The Inn and the mansion were used to entertain lavish guests, which included presidents, actors and famous musicians. Jones held the title of the property until his death in 1927. His wife, Alice, held the property together using the help of staff and friends until she also passed in 1931.

By that time, Jones's daughter, Sallie Jones Sexton, had just graduated college. Sallie was offered a job at *Time* magazine, but she missed her old home too much. Following the death of her parents, Sallie decided to move back to the mansion and take over the property. While living in the mansion, Sallie put herself in charge of running the Granville Inn, where she became quite the local celebrity. She had a foul mouth and a charismatic personality. She was known for her bubbly demeanor and unladylike behavior that some saw as charming and others found repulsive. She was married for only two years to James Joseph Sexton Jr., and after their divorce, Sallie never remarried. She became too preoccupied with her career as a show horse trainer to properly manage the Inn, which eventually led to bankruptcy.

The property was then sold to William and Ortha Wright, who turned the property into a restaurant, before being sold again to Quest International to be used as the nonprofit's headquarters. Once Quest International relocated to Newark in 1994, the property was sold to Dave Longaberger. Longaberger renovated the current property and added new buildings before passing away just before the new decade. In 2004, the Granville Village Council created the Bryn Du Commission, which still cares for the property to this day.

Today, the Bryn Du Mansion is a public space that can be rented for various uses. The property has been used to host weddings, community events, music events and trade shows. Bryn Du even has art events and art classes offered in the space as well. The fifty-two acres of the property make for an amazing venue for both public and private uses. However, the most common events that take place at Bryn Du aren't the weddings or the receptions but rather the ghost hunts! You can choose to attend

The Granville Inn sits right across the street from the Buxton Inn.

either private or public ghost hunts at the mansion for one of the cheapest admission tickets to any paranormal hot spot in central Ohio. The old mansion housed many families over its time, and as you probably could have guessed, some of them have yet to leave.

The most common sighting is the spirit of Sallie Jones Sexton herself. The property is used for weddings fairly often, and with weddings comes pictures. Over the past two decades, dozens of reports have been shared of wedding photographs that have an apparition of an unknown woman in an old-fashioned dress somewhere on the property. Sometimes she can be seen through the windows of the buildings, while other times she has been standing right next to members of the families being photographed for the wedding album. When paranormal teams have gone in to investigate the mansion, they tend to capture EVPs of a woman's voice. They have also captured ghostly figures of a woman in mirrors and standing in doorways.

Sallie doesn't seem to be alone on the property. Other investigators have reported seeing unexplainable balls of light, what would typically be described as orbs, that appear and disappear without explanation inside the mansion's bedrooms. Photos of apparitions that greatly resemble John Sutphin Jones have been captured as well. While alone in the house, people have heard heavy footsteps walking through the hallways and bedrooms when no one is there to make them. A deep, disembodied male voice is sometimes heard throughout the property or captured on voice recording devices.

Above: Bryn Du Mansion consists of a massive estate sitting on almost fifty-three acres of land.

Right: Visitors and paranormal teams have seen ghostly figures in the windows and on the balcony of Bryn Du Mansion for years.

Most of the paranormal teams that have investigated the Bryn Du Mansion and posted their gathered evidence online seem to have similar experiences. Equipment will go off on its own, batteries will be drained, electromagnetic field readers will spike, temperatures will dramatically rise and fall with unexplainable causes and doors will be opened or closed on their own. Staff members of the building have had strange occurrences as well, most of the time without the witness having any knowledge of the paranormal happenings of the venue. A caterer of a public event back in 2014 had written a review about her experience. She described setting up tables and chairs to hold food before an event had started. As she glanced up from the table, she saw a man standing in the window looking out at her from around a curtain. The man's face was completely expressionless, so she stared back at him, puzzled. Within just a matter of seconds, the man disappeared, and the caterer was left shocked and speechless. It is safe to say that if you plan on investigating the mansion or holding some kind of event on the property, you definitely should avoid walking around alone.

The Bryn Du mansion is a beautiful and large space that is rich in history. It is an amazing venue to use the next time that you need to gather your loved ones. Don't let the ghost stories scare you away from the opportunity to experience the property. Or better yet, make a trip to come investigate the mansion for yourself. Surely Sallie would love to make your acquaintance. She might even want to get a photo together.

Something in the Water

When someone comes forward to claim themselves as a paranormal investigator, most skeptics will snicker and say something along the lines of "Oh, like the Ghostbusters?"—all to make a joke out of the situation. Paranormal investigation has had a long past of being seen as silly or childish, until recent years, when the desire to watch paranormal investigations unfold on TV has risen. As technology advances, the living have developed more clear and concise ways of communicating with the dead. To put it simply, the Ghostbusters are to ghosts as Terminix is to ants and termites. In the movies, they show up in their funny suits and use industry-specific equipment to rid your house of spirits and monsters.

Real-life ghost hunters, or paranormal investigation teams, are more scientific than that. They arrive on the scene and use any equipment possible to establish patterns of unexplainable behavior. Investigators must go into every investigation with a clear mind and a reasonable amount of skepticism. If the behavior can be explained away, then it must be considered normal or explainable behavior. Once the behavior cannot be explained as normal, especially after being unable to find the natural cause of the activity, then it can be deemed as paranormal. Once the paranormal behavior acts in a pattern, it can be described as a haunting. The next step is to investigate the haunting to discover what type of haunting it is. If it is an intelligent haunting, then the investigators will be able to communicate with it using the new technology of the era.

Over the past few decades, these researchers have gotten much better results and created much stronger theories due to the new devices that can be used to study paranormal happenings. We now have high-quality cameras and video recorders to capture images of spirits or to record and prove to others that devices were going off without explanation. There are K2 readers, or EMF readers, that measure electromagnetic fields, which help investigators become aware of a spirit's presence. There are REM pods that light up and make noise whenever anything gets too close to the antenna and disturbs the electromagnetic field that it gives off. The development of thermal technology allows people to take note of any rises or drops in temperature, as well as thermal imaging that can capture the outline of spirits that are not visible with the naked eye. Voice recording devices are able to hear the messages of the dead that human ears cannot detect. The human ear can only hear sounds between certain frequencies, but technology allows for investigators to capture voices from beyond the grave that can be played back and studied.

Investigators try to speak with the spirits and ask them questions regarding what life is like after death, or at least in the state of existence that they are currently in. They want to discover what the spirits can remember about their lives, how they experience the world as a spirit and why they are still here. If the information shared by the spirit can be confirmed based on real, documented history, then there is solid evidence that life does not end after death. But with that discovery only comes more questions, and we might not learn the answer to those questions until our technology develops even more to help us experience the afterlife in a greater depth.

Investigators will tell you that the most common hauntings are what the industry refers to as "residual hauntings." In fact, a large percent of all paranormal happenings can fall into this category. The severity of residual hauntings can vary. Some residual hauntings can be so shocking that it leaves the ones who bear witness to it forever traumatized. Other residual hauntings can be happening right under your nose without being noticed. Residual hauntings are best described as events that are stuck in a time loop and continuously repeat themselves. It's as if someone pauses a recorded video, rewinds the footage, and plays the tape again, over and over. Residual hauntings would appear as seeing an apparition of a person walking down the stairs every night at the same time or music being played without a source every night. If a person dies in a house fire and the new property built on the land regularly experiences unexplainable smells of smoke, then that would be considered a residual haunting.

The causes for these types of hauntings is still somewhat unknown, but most paranormal researchers have the same theory. If an event that is traumatic, violent or emotional in nature occurs in a location, then a blast of negative energy can be sent out into the surrounding area. That negative energy has so much power and emotion to it that even after the event ends and the people involved move on, the area still echoes the activity throughout time. Some residual hauntings might not even be visible. Some of the best evidence of a residual haunting is the unexplainable occurrence of smells and sounds, like smelling old-fashioned perfume or cigar smoke or hearing footsteps with no one being around to cause them. People living in a home with a residual haunting will experience very mild, sometimes hardly noticeable, activity that repeats itself regularly.

Visual residual hauntings are not nearly as common, which is why the fact that Licking County has so many of them is all the more intriguing. What's even stranger is that most of them seem to be related to water in one way or another. Researchers have theories that paranormal activity is more prevalent "on a dark and stormy night" because of the moisture in the air and the static electricity. Since water is a great conductor of electricity, the two go hand in hand, and electricity is very common in hauntings. Spirits have been known to drain batteries of electronic devices in order to gain the energy to manifest in some way. EMF readers are the most common paranormal investigation tool because the presence of a ghost can set off the device the same way the electricity does. Water can conduct for the paranormal just the same way it does for electricity.

Back in the day, most of Ohio was a swamp. A lot of water had to be drained or rerouted to create space for farms and homes. In Licking County, there are many lakes, ponds, streams, rivers and underground water sources that have been around for as long as recorded history. This water seems to be holding on to the negative energy of tragic events and causing a bewildering number of residual hauntings. Union Township, one of twenty-five townships in the county, has a massive lake that is known to be haunted. The official name of the lake is Union Lake, but that is not what the residents of the township call it. It was renamed by the locals of the area to Hell Lake and has been called that ever since the 1960s. Hell Lake got its name because of the residual haunting that occurs there. An apparition of a young boy is seen floating in the water. He appears just before sunset and will float from one end of the lake to the other. The identity of who the boy is and what happened to him is unknown. Given the nature of the haunting, it is widely believed that the boy drowned in the lake in life.

Another well-known haunting involving water is a spirit that has been dubbed "Swamp Road Sally." Swamp Road is a road in Licking County that crosses over Slim Creek. The road itself is not very long, with a small bridge that passes over the creek. Swamp Road was originally built back in the 1830s. The road was passing through what was then known as Pigeon Swamp, one of the very many swamps in the state. The early settlers would pile dirt up high enough to construct a road that would be elevated out of the swamp and create more infrastructure for the area. Once the surrounding towns became more established, the swamp was drained, and the water was relocated to aid in the creation of the Ohio-Erie Canal.

The origin story of where Swamp Road Sally came from varies from person to person. The premise of the story is that Sally was a girl who was involved in a horrible and fatal car accident on that road. The collision was so bad that she was ejected from her vehicle and landed in the swampland on the side of the road. Ever since this infamous accident, sightings of Sally have been reported. The most common story is that of drivers having to slam on their breaks to avoid hitting a woman that walks from one side of the road to the other before disappearing into thin air. Other people have shared personal experiences of getting out of their vehicles to explore the road and see what they can discover about Sally.

Some of them report hearing the faint sound of crying and sobbing in the darkness on the side of the road. It is speculated that the sound might be a residual haunting of Sally lying on the damp and muddy earth, sobbing in pain from her accident before she passed on. One story involving Sally

Earth was collected and packed together to elevate Swamp Road out of the swamp it used to sit in.

The long stretch of road that Swamp Road Sally walks at night.

recounts a time when a group of friends were driving down Swamp Road when suddenly the car shuts off. The car came to a stop, and the driver was unable to start the vehicle back up. The passengers urged the driver to resolve the issue, as anxiety began to take hold of them. What could be more dangerous than being stuck in the middle of a dark road with no lights on? As the teens tried to find a source of the malfunction, they heard the sound of a vehicle slamming on its breaks and the screeching of tires as a driver tried to bring the vehicle to a stop. The sound was so loud that the group was certain that they were about to feel the impact of a collision from the rear of the car. However, as everyone braced for impact, nothing happened. The teens sat in confusion, and one of them got out of the car to look around. There were no other vehicles on the road for as far as they could see. All of a sudden, their car roared back to life. Startled beyond words, the group took off as fast as they could, trying desperately to put as much distance between themselves and the road as possible.

The legend of Black Hand Gorge and the legend of the Captain's Ghost also have very strong ties to water, more specifically the Ohio-Erie Canal. Many laborers who built the canals had passed away during the project due to diseases that were being spread through the bugs of the swamps and terrain. Maybe all the spiritually tainted water that runs throughout the entire state of Ohio is the fuel that keeps these legends alive and the spirits active. Hopefully someday, we will be able to lay these spirits to rest. But until that day, Licking County, stay away from the water.

ARE WE ALONE?

It's human nature to be curious. Since the early stages of man, humanity as a species has been asking questions and testing theories in order to better understand what is happening around us. Children for all of recorded history have had a "why?" phase that causes them to question what they see. This inquisitive nature seems to be a survival tactic, which has served our species well, since it has led to the modern-day science and technology that we use and forever continue to expand on. However, even with all of the technology that we have developed so far, there are still two things about our reality that we can't seem to get a firm grasp on. Firstly, our own oceans—we have no idea what's really down there! And secondly, outer space.

Mankind turned its gaze to the stars millennia ago, and we haven't been able to look away since. In our early days, we tracked the patterns of the sun, moon and stars in order to create calendars. We created patterns in the night sky and created astrology and the concept of the zodiac. We made inventions such as the telescope and satellites in order to get a better view of the galaxy and other celestial bodies around us. Our curiosity has had the best of us for generations, and we keep craving to discover more and more. But the more we learn, the more questions we have. Scientists discovered some time ago that the universe is expanding and always has been since its creation. The universe is bigger than absolutely anything anyone can fathom, beyond all human comprehension. There are more planets in the universe than blades of grass on our planet. Through these discoveries, the most popular question to ever arise has been on the minds of billions of people throughout history:

Are we alone? Are there other forms of intelligent life in existence, and will we ever be able to make contact with them? Well, some would argue that we already have.

Alien sightings have been reported for thousands of years. Some of the earliest human artwork has shown designs of other lifeforms or advanced flying objects. There are many theories surrounding when mankind made its first contact with extraterrestrial life. Some state that alien lifeforms helped build the Egyptian pyramids and other fascinating wonders of the world. People cannot understand how ancient civilizations were able to build such large and advanced structures using the limited technology of the time. One theory states that aliens first arrived after the explosions of the nuclear bombs dropped during World War II, in an effort to prevent mankind from releasing harmful nuclear fallout into the atmosphere and outer space. Some other theories state that aliens and the human race really began to work together during the Cold War. About 57 percent of people believe that some type of alien race exists, and most alien fanatics believe that the U.S. government, specifically the CIA, is operating with a plan to hide aliens and evidence of extraterrestrial life. People believe that the CIA's reasoning for hiding the evidence of alien life is to prevent widespread panic or to build relationships with them to learn scientific and military advanced technology.

Please keep in mind that most information provided in this conspiracy theory is alleged and should not be taken as fact. The first report of an unidentified flying saucer in the United States occurred on June 24, 1947, by a pilot who was in the air searching for a crashed plane. After that report, many military pilots and officers began reporting strange activity while doing test flights, combat exercises and drills, and watching radars. By the start of 1948, air force general Nathan Twining had created Project SIGN, which was to gather, study, and share any information or sightings of alien life with other government organizations. Project SIGN began its work at Wright-Patterson Air Force Base in Dayton, Ohio. The air force used Project SIGN to announce that all information gathered about UFOs were not legitimate claims. The reports that were coming in were explained away as having normal causes or were scrutinized to be fake, but reports continued to be filed from military members, law enforcement officials and the general public.

As tensions rose with the Soviet Union and during the Korean War, the USAF director of intelligence established Project Blue Book in 1952. Project Blue Book was created to investigate the UFO sightings that had more validity and had the potential of being an actual sighting of an alien specimen. It is theorized that Project Blue Book was created and overseen by a group of high-ranking military officials and given strict orders to exclude any information of extraterrestrial life from the general public and the president of the country. Any citizen of the United States could run for president, hold the office for a maximum of eight years and then retire from the position while knowing all of the government's most precious secrets. Handling an alien species that is far more advanced than our own was too delicate of a matter to leave in the hands of whoever won the title of president and who wouldn't stay longer than a few years. To maintain order and attempt to avoid worldwide panic, the information regarding any communication and deals made with alien lifeforms would stay among the military and the CIA, who held much more permanent positions of authority. After Project Book's launch, the United States had a huge surge of scientific breakthroughs and advancements. The military technology of the nation was improving much faster than it ever had before. Alien theorists believe that the CIA made a deal with an alien race that would allow them to abduct U.S. citizens for study and testing in exchange for information on advanced flight mechanics and weaponry that would be tested at Area 51 in Nevada.

In addition to scientific breakthroughs, the number of reported UFO sightings and alien abductions have absolutely skyrocketed since the Cold War. Most reports that come in from the United States seem to come from relatively quiet and remote areas, such as Alaska, Vermont, Maine, Montana, New Mexico and Arizona. However, in recent years, a large number of reports have been flooding in from the state of Ohio, more specifically cities in Licking County. But why here?

Alien enthusiasts of central Ohio have theorized that Licking County has been seeing an increase of UFO activity due to the earthworks in Newark, Ohio. The earthworks are nearly 1,500 years old, and historians today still have a very loose idea of what they were actually used for. The native tribes that created them cleared out hundreds and hundreds of acres of trees and moved dirt just to create an absolutely massive flat and clear land. Then they would create large mounds in the shape of patterns that can only be seen from very high up in the air. Some of the circles are so big that an entire Egyptian pyramid can fit inside of one, and there are dozens of these circles and lines connecting them that run for miles. Modern-day pilots are able to see the earthworks from thousands of feet in the air, and all of the time, work and detail that was put into them is clearly visible. Who, 1,500 years ago, would be a few miles in the air and looking down on these earthworks? Were they created as a work of art for the gods, or were the tribes creating

The prehistoric Newark earthworks are protected and funded by local government and historic societies.

some sort of landing pad for any alien species that was visiting them? Many storytellers of the tribes, even to this day, tell stories of gods that descended to earth from huge flying contraptions, far beyond anything these people have ever seen before or since, and the stories are not told as mythology. The stories of being visited by these beings from somewhere in the heavens is documented as part of their real recorded history. Maybe the increase in UFO sightings is because an alien race is returning to the earthworks that were built for them. This theory is heavily countered by historic societies in the area and historians who work specifically on Native American cultures. These people believe that the earthworks were sacred places for ceremonies and nothing more.

More recently, UFO sightings have been on the rise in Newark. In 2015, a video went viral and even made it onto the local news network of a large, orange, diamond-shaped UFO flying through the night sky. The best way to describe the shape is that it looked similar to the Millennium Falcon from the Star Wars franchise, only pointed in the rear rather than rounded. The object was seen flying through the night sky before coming to a stop and vanishing. In addition to UFO sightings, reports of alien abductions have been increasing all throughout Licking County since the mid-1990s. The stories of abductions and visitations have been so abundant that entire webpages and forums have been created for people to share their experiences.

One report from Pataskala, Ohio, tells a story of a driver coming home after visiting family in Columbus late one night when the vehicle lost all power. As the car came to a stop, the driver put the vehicle in park and turned

Top: Massive mounds and deep trenches that go on for miles in mysterious shapes were constructed by the prehistoric Hopewell tribe.

Bottom: The earthworks were giant circles and designs that historians believe were used to create sacred spaces to conduct ceremonies.

the ignition off. When they tried to restart the vehicle, nothing happened. Just before getting out to look under the hood, a bright light engulfed the car from above. The light was so bright that it was nearly blinding. The driver covered their eyes and turned their head toward the passenger seat. After what only felt like a few seconds, the light vanished, and the vehicle roared to life again. The driver, confused and scared, continued on their path home. After a few minutes of trying to rationalize the event that just took place, the driver glanced at the clock on the dashboard to discover that three hours of time had passed in what felt like just a few minutes. After trying to come up with an explanation, the driver theorized that the clock must have malfunctioned during the electrical phenomenon. They continued their drive and arrived home shortly after. Before going to bed, the driver glanced at the bedside alarm clock, just to find that this clock *also* read three hours ahead of the time that it should be. In an absolutely terrified and confused state, the driver decided to go to bed. To this day, they cannot explain what had happened to them logically.

If you are an alien enthusiast in Licking County, you luckily won't have to travel very far to fuel your hobby. New videos of UFO sightings are posted online every month, and new personal experiences with aliens and other extraterrestrial, paranormal happenings are shared almost every day. There are tons of chat rooms, forums, blogs and websites where you can go to share your encounters or hear the stories that others have to share. If you ever decide to go alien hunting, try your best to get your experiences on video. With all the skeptics out there, you need all the proof you can gather to convince someone that, no, we are absolutely not alone in this universe.

Black Eyed Children

Have you ever been sitting at home when someone knocks on your door or rings your doorbell, but you aren't expecting anyone, so you ignore it until the uninvited guests leave? This has become a fairly common practice among the millennial and younger generations because sometimes it can be scary to answer the door. If you aren't expecting someone, you have no idea who's out there. It could be an annoying door-to-door salesman, an angry neighbor with bad news that you don't want to hear or a political party that wants to persuade your opinion in the upcoming election. Or even worse, what if it is a murderer or some kind of monster out to get you? No, that can't be it. That would be absurd…right?

There is a relatively new urban legend that is actually becoming fairly widespread throughout the world. Black eyed children, also sometimes referred to as Black Eyed Kids, or BEK, were first reported in other countries in the early 1970s. Reports popped up here and there throughout the world, with little attention being paid to them, until one particular case occurred in Abilene, Texas, covered by a journalist named Brian Bethel in the mid-'90s. Bethel came forward and shared a story of the night he was approached by a pair of black eyed children. Bethel was sitting, parked in his vehicle in a parking lot while he was writing a check when two boys approached his driver-side window. One of the boys knocked on his window, and as Bethel began to roll his window down, he noticed that his entire body was almost instantly filled with a sense of utter dread and terror, even though he could not understand why. He didn't feel threatened by the kids, and he was feeling fine just a moment ago, so he couldn't explain where the shaking hands, pit in his stomach and overwhelming sense of fear was coming from. The older of the two boys, using a hood to cover the top half of his face and his head tilted down, told Bethel that they needed a ride home to get some money so they could see a movie. The boy followed his request by pointing out that they were just two harmless kids and they "didn't have a gun or anything," so Bethel should have no issue with giving them a ride back home.

The boy's choice of wording struck Bethel as being completely odd. Not to mention, his body's fight-or-flight response hit its peak, with all the hairs on his body standing up since the moment he noticed the kids. Bethel looked away from the children and began coming up with excuses as to why he would not be able to give them a ride. When he looked back at the kids, the boys were staring him right in the eye. He immediately noticed that they had very pale, ghostly white skin, and their eyes were completely black. The entire eye, top to bottom, left to right, was as dark as an onyx gem, with no white portion showing at all. While Bethel froze in fear, the older child aggressively responded, stating that they could not enter his car until he told them that they were allowed to. At this point, Bethel rolled up the window and tore out of the parking lot as fast as he could. To this day, he assures that this story is true.

Ever since Brian's story, people all over the United States have come forward sharing times that they had strange encounters with black eyed children. The stories usually take place in a confined space, like a house, business or car. In almost every circumstance, at least two or more children will approach the witness wearing hoods or hats or looking down at the ground. They will always state some type of emergency, like losing their parents, being lost and needing to borrow a phone or being injured and needing medical attention. They will request access to the witness's home or vehicle. Nearly every person that has a black eyed children story will say that their body can practically sense the danger of these children when in their presence. The hairs on their entire body stand up, and they become overwhelmed with a feeling of fear, even if they can't rationally explain why. This panicked feeling will cause most people to deny the children, but the kids always persist. They will beg, demand or even threaten the witness to try to gain access to their space. A handful of reporters have said that they closed the door in the children's face, just for them to start loudly pounding on the door. At some point during these encounters, the children will look at the witness, and that is when they will see that the kids all have solid black eyes on a pale, expressionless face. If the children get denied enough, they will go away, but they will never enter the space without an invitation.

Very little is known about what happens to those who actually let the children inside. A few cases report that the children came inside only for a brief moment or two before leaving, but then the occupants of the home will experience horrible health conditions following that night. Reports have included nose bleeds, long-lasting migraines, strokes, heart attacks and even sudden symptoms of cancer that later lead to a diagnosis. Other people have said that once the children have entered their home, they disappeared into thin air, only for the home to begin showing signs that it is haunted. Items will be unexplainably moved or go missing, people have been pushed out of their bed or down the stairs, closet doors are ripped open violently and disembodied sounds of child laughter are heard throughout the house. In extreme cases, the residents of the home have had horrifying nightmares that they can't control or wake up from. They have also shared having unexplainable out-of-body experiences where their spirit will leave their physical body and they can't seem to get back in. The people who claim to have experienced this express that the event is the most terrifying thing they have ever experienced, that it feels too real to just be a dream. They have coherent and collected thoughts and are able to recall what other people in the house were doing accurately, in real time, while their body was asleep in bed. A few missing persons reports have involved family and friends coming to the police and stating that the missing person had called them just after having a strange encounter with children at their front door just days, or sometimes hours, before being reported missing. This creates another theory that once the black eyed children enter a home, they abduct the occupants and do…whatever they do with them.

It's safe to say that you don't want to find out what exactly happens when you let these children into your home, car or place of work. These occurrences have begun happening so recently that not enough investigation has been done to better understand what these things are. Many theories have been thrown around, based on what has been reported so far. Most modern alien abduction claims involve the extracting of reproductive cells, so some people theorize that the kids are alien-human hybrids. That would explain their alien-like eyes, lack of social skills and poor choice of words when attempting to convince their victims to take pity on them. As for their speed and disappearances, the alien theory predicts that they are actually using teleportation. Another theory about these kids is that they are born vampires. Evidence for this claim is due to the age-old folklore that vampires need to be invited into the space of their victims in order to claim them. This would also explain their complexion and their speed of disappearing. The last theory is that the children are some sort of spirit or fae. This theory arose due to the majority of cases where the witness allowed the children into their homes, resulting in the children disappearing into thin air and a haunting ensuing after.

Either the children have been coming around more often, or more people feel more comfortable sharing experiences that they once thought they would keep private for the rest of their lives, as sightings of black eyed children have been on the rise all over the United States and specifically in Pataskala, Ohio. One report was shared on a paranormal Ohio Reddit forum from a mother who was in her vehicle with her child. After visiting the Pataskala Municipal Park, just down the road from Pataskala Cemetery, the mother put her daughter in the backseat before climbing into the driver's seat and starting her vehicle. The sun had just started to set, and she was planning on taking her daughter for ice cream before heading home. Just as the engine roared to life, a young girl knocked on her driver side door. She looked to be about seven or eight years old, the same age as her daughter, and she was flanked by three older boys, maybe between the ages of ten and twelve. The boys were turned inward to face one another in a circle, while the young girl looked down at her feet as she spoke to the driver. The girl said that she and her brothers came to the park with their mom, but now they couldn't find her. The little girl asked the woman to give them a ride home. The woman was concerned for the kids, but for some strange and unexplainable reason, she had a pit in her stomach and an unbearable feeling of dread. The young mother asked the girl if she knew her mom's phone number so they could call her and ask where she went. According to the post, the little girl looked up and stared directly at the woman, which revealed that her eyes were completely black. In a frustrated tone, the girl demanded that she let them in her car. By now, the boys had moved to the front of the vehicle and stared at the woman through the windshield, also with eyes as black as coal. Immediately, the mother put her car in reverse and sped out of the parking lot, heading straight home and telling her husband all about the encounter. He didn't believe her, stating that she was trying to scare him. The woman held that story in her heart as a secret for years, wondering if she had imagined the whole thing and doubting her sanity, until she began to hear the stories of others who witnessed the black eyed children too.

Another report comes from July 2010, in Newark, Ohio. A security guard working a night shift decided to take a cigarette break and headed outside.

The parking lot to Pataskala Municipal Park, where a local woman claims to have been approached by a group of black eyed children.

He noticed a group of teenagers across the street who were looking over in his direction with completely black eyes. He quickly finished his cigarette and headed back inside, locking the door behind him. When he returned to his desk and glanced at the security cameras, he noticed that the boys were standing right outside the front entrance. One of the boys was motioning through the security cameras for him to come to the door. The guard approached the front door and asked what the kids wanted through the glass. One of the teenagers said that they needed to use his phone and requested that he let them in, which he declined. When the security guard returned to his desk, he noticed that the first boy was still looking at him, through the security camera at the front door, while the other two had moved to the back door. They seemed to be looking directly into his eyes, as if they could see him through the camera, just as well as he could see them. As the guard grew more and more afraid, he decided to call the police. When the officer arrived, he searched the entire perimeter of the building and could not find the teenagers anywhere, even though the security guard never looked away from the video feed. The teenagers simply vanished into thin air.

Part of what makes this legend so scary is that the antagonists are young children. Back in the day, children were hardly seen as people. They were simply side characters that existed to help with household chores and work. Through the Industrial Revolution, child labor was used to help clear blockages in the machines. Children were small enough to crawl into the big machines, and while they'd sometimes lose fingers or entire limbs from unsafe work environments, it wasn't seen as a big issue for a long time. It wasn't until the child evangelism movement of the 1930s that society's views on children changed. No longer were they just little things that could be put to use. Evangelicals stressed the importance of the nuclear family and sought to portray children as a symbol of innocence. The ideas of "childlike wonder" and pure-heartedness were shared with parents, and child labor laws were advocated for before being placed in effect. Ever since then, children, specifically between the ages of four and fourteen, have been viewed as precious gems that need to be protected and cherished. They were gifts, given to the parents by God. It was from this pure image that the idea of a most horrifying evil came to fruition: the child villain.

Horror novels and movies started to be written in a way that depicted an adorable child who is as sweet as honey, who turns out to be a psychotic murderer, the child of the devil, the antichrist, possessed by demons or anything else that would cause harm. What made these books and movies so scary was that it felt like the killer was betraying the audience. With the child's soft eyes and heartwarming smile, it came as such a surprise when he or she would cause such harm to others and be able to get away with it—no one would suspect that such an innocent child could be capable of such horrible things. An example of this would include the movie *The Good Son*, starring Macaulay Culkin, where he plays a child psychopath. Culkin's character is shown throughout the movie slowly showing more dangerous signs of psychopathic behavior. The young boy kills a dog, seriously injures his sister in an attempt to kill her and even attempts to murder his own mother before being stopped by the protagonist. Whenever someone tries to report what is happening or get help from an outsider to put a stop to his madness, the child is able to put on an innocent act and convince the rest of the town that he is harmless. Another example would be the movie *Orphan*, from 2009. In this movie, an adult woman poses as a nine-year-old adopted girl and attempts to murder her new adoptive mother in order to take her place in the family. The movie is critically acclaimed, and you can find it on any horror movie fan's top ten favorites list because the suspenseful twist of the movie caught first-time viewers by surprise.

The idea of children using their newfound innocence and vulnerability to lure in unsuspecting victims is a relatively new concept, but it surely is effective in giving people a good scare. Maybe the reports of the black eyed children are just mass hysteria or a fun story that people came up with in order to scare one another. Or maybe there really is a group of alien-human hybrids or newborn vampires or wandering lost souls that are out there posing as defenseless children in an attempt to claim another victim. It will never be confirmed unless the new generation of paranormal investigators can get on the scene and start uncovering the mystery behind these strange appearances. According to many online forums, Licking County seems like a great place to start! If you are a resident of Pataskala Ohio, do your best to keep yourself safe. Keep your doors locked, your windows shut and your vehicle secured. And if strange children ever show up on your doorstep, demanding entry to your home, be firm. Get a good look at their eyes, and if anything seems fishy or if your body is warning you of danger, listen to your instincts. Don't ever, ever, let a black eyed child into your home. You might not live to tell the tale.

Hell Is In Ohio

Recent studies show that 78 percent of people living in the United States claim to follow some type of religion. About 65 percent of that is Christianity or some close variation of it. These statistics make sense, seeing as the first settlers to arrive here from Europe were fleeing from religious persecution or trying to create a home by living a Puritan lifestyle. Religion drives people in many ways to do a lot of things. People love to be a part of a like-minded group and feel a sense of community, and religion tends to provide that for most people. But having strong faith can also lead to problems, such as seen during the witch trials that spread all throughout Europe and the colonies out of fear of the devil. Shortly after the end of the trials, officials of the city and of the church admitted that they reacted out of fear of the demonic and cleared the names of the victims of the witch hunt. Historians look back at that period, study how the mass hysteria caused so much chaos and wonder how people could get so wrapped up in something so silly, but have you ever noticed that the panic from those trials never really seemed to end?

Christianity teaches of a loving God and a wicked devil who are constantly in a spiritual clash, and their followers here on earth are soldiers in that army. That is why when people do kind acts, such as volunteering for the needy, healing the sick or uplifting someone emotionally, it is referred to as "doing the work of God." Conversely, for many decades, people have also shamed and criticized things that have been viewed as unholy or satanic. The idea was relatively tame until the 1960s, when equal rights activist groups became far more active. As women became more liberated, LGBT people began fighting for respect and the hippie movement was on the rise, the people who favored the old-fashioned and conservative way of life started to fear that the devil was influencing the youth to turn against the word of God. Kids of the time were experimenting with drugs such as marijuana, ecstasy and LSD. Rock music became more popular, with lyrics about sex, drugs, partying and breaking the rules. People started getting tattoos more frequently, which was seen as ungodly for a long time and is sometimes still being criticized today. With the progression of the LGBT rights movement, more and more people were openly expressing their love and sexuality. All of these social changes shocked evangelicals and the members of old-fashioned conservative America. These people were taught their whole lives that these acts were sinful, and they were concerned that their children were going to be "corrupted" by these behaviors into going against God.

This fear created what is known as the Satanic Panic of the '70s, even though the real panic started setting in during the 1980s. The Satanic Panic was, and still is, a loose movement of hyper-religious Christians who believe that Satan and his followers are influencing the media to slowly corrupt people into going against the church and doing the devil's work. This panic escalated due to the Manson family murders. During the hippie movement, it became somewhat common to see people gathering to create compounds, communities or small nomadic groups and living a lifestyle vastly different from mainstream society. After the actions of Charles Manson and his family made front-page news, most people caught up in the Satanic Panic were convinced that *all* of these communities were under an evil influence. Even police began to believe that cults of Satan worshippers were living in caves and tunnels underground and performing rituals and sacrifices in his name. Law enforcement being tainted by these fears actually caused criminal cases to be handled improperly. The most famous case to be influenced by the Satanic Panic was the case of the West Memphis Three.

On May 5, 1993, in West Memphis, Arkansas, three sets of parents called into the local police department to inform law enforcement that their eight-year-old sons had gone missing. The kids were last seen riding their bikes around 6:00 p.m. but never made it back home. The next morning, police found the bodies of the boys in a ditch near Robin Hood Hills. The bodies were recovered out of the water completely naked, with their hands tied to their ankles with shoelaces, with scars and mutilation marks all over them. After the discovery, rumors started that the culprits must have been from a devil-worshipping cult in the area. Police immediately began investigating the slightest link between the murders and local cult activity. The next day, police questioned seventeen-year-old Damien Echols about the murders. Despite the fact that Damien had a solid alibi of being home that night with his mother while talking on the phone with a young lady, he was still suspected of the murder due to his Gothic lifestyle. Damien was going through a difficult period of his life, dealing with depression and other psychiatric problems, and he was very troubled because of it. He was known for having long hair, dressing in black, writing Gothic-style poems and practicing Wicca. A few months prior to the murders, Echols was committed to a psychiatric ward and placed on suicide watch for his well-being. Once he got home to West Memphis, he was meeting regularly with a social worker.

Investigators questioned Echols multiple times and convinced themselves that he was lying about not knowing anything about the murders. They also began questioning one of his friends, who had the same tattoo on his hand as Echols. The friend's name was Jason Baldwin, and he also repeatedly told investigators that he didn't know anything about the murders. But the detectives didn't believe him. The police did not have any evidence that linked either of the boys to the murders. Their appearance led people to believe that they were devil worshipers, and their hobbies and interests led people to assume that they were psychopaths and dangers to society. Law enforcement wanted to rush through the case in order to ease the worries of the community, but the investigation started to wind down. That is, until a random waitress, Vicki Hutcheson, came to the police asking to play detective because she wanted to bring the suspected cultists to justice. Vicki lived next to another seventeen-year-old boy named Jessie Misskelley, who had a lower-than-average IQ. Misskelley was friends with Echols, and Vicki was hoping to use Misskelley to meet with Echols, grow close to him and try to discover if he had involvement in the murders.

Vicki Hutcheson told a story, which she later revealed to be not true, of Echols driving her and Misskelley in a red Ford Escape to a meeting of witches. Echols never had a car and didn't drive anyone else's vehicle, which he and his family tried mentioning multiple times during the case. In Vicki's story, they were taken to a field outside town and met with multiple other young people who had their faces and arms painted black. As the group started doing cult-like activity, Vicki asked Echols to take her home, which he did, but he left Misskelley at the scene. Police used this story to bring Jessie Misskelley in for questioning. They reminded him that there was a $35,000 reward for helping with the investigation that would go to his family if he was able to help them close the case. As they polygraph tested Misskelley, he explained how he knew nothing about the murders and that he was never involved with a cult or any other satanic activity. However, due to his different appearance and his friendship with another troubled teen, the detectives refused to believe that he was innocent. Police would ask him questions about what happened with the boys, since they supposedly knew that he was involved with their deaths. Misskelley would tell them what he had heard what happened to the boys from the news. Detectives asked him what they were tied with, and Misskelley answered that it was a rope. The detectives yelled at Misskelley about "playing dumb" and told him that he knew that they were tied with shoelaces. Then they asked Misskelley again what was used to tie up the boys, and he would reply with the correct answer. Jessie also said that he thought that the murders took place during the day, but the detectives yelled at him more and informed him that they happened at night. The detectives continued to groom him and feed Jessie the correct answers to their questions until he was able to repeat back to them exactly what was known about the case. Once he was able to repeat what had happened at the scene, the detectives filmed Misskelley describing the accounts and called it a confession.

With this fabricated confession, Jessie Misskelley, Damien Echols and Jason Baldwin were arrested for the murders. They stood trial, where the lack of proper evidence and inconsistency of stories were ignored by the jury, who judged the appearance and mental health issues of the teens as obvious signs of occult activity. The three of them were convicted and wrongfully sentenced to prison. They served about fifteen years for a crime they had absolutely no part of until new evidence surfaced. After a call for justice from the public, the case was reviewed, and the West Memphis Three were released from prison in 2011. This case is brought up all the time when discussing how senseless fear of the occult in a community could cause horrible outcomes. The West Memphis Three were teenagers with hobbies that ostracized them. They read Stephen King, liked tattoos, had long hair, wrote dark poetry and were struggling with their emotions and their mental health. The town saw that as an obvious sign that they were devil-worshipping murderers who didn't have an innocent bone in their body. The Satanic Panic that swept this town in Arkansas took years of life away from three people that they will never be able to get back. However, you can understand why the police and the neighborhood were so afraid of the situation. The circumstances around the deaths of those young boys were horrific. What if a cult really had committed those crimes? We now know that that wasn't the case because no such cult was operating in that area, but could such a cult exist somewhere else?

The Satanic Panic has always been around Ohio, and that is mostly due to the fact that a lot of satanic or cult activity has been happening in the state for a long time. In 1985, Union County in Central Ohio was having an issue with mutilated remains of animals popping up everywhere. Nearly two hundred animal carcasses were found in parks, on the streets and in playgrounds. The bodies would oftentimes be headless or have strange markings and drawings cut into the animal's skin. The grave of a Civil War soldier was also dug up and tampered with. A deputy in Marysville at the time claimed that the best lead that the Sheriff's Department had was that a cult that worshipped the devil was operating in the area.

Ohio also had its own share of witch accusations back in the day. One witch hunt happened in Cleveland when an old lady by the last name of Stoskopf murdered her husband and children and threw their bodies down a well. She was accused of being a witch and hanged for her crimes. She was buried at Myrtle Hill Cemetery, but in a very peculiar way. They laid her body feet first and buried her standing straight up. For her headstone, they placed a giant stone ball right on top of where her head was, to make sure that the demonic witch would never be able to escape the earth she was buried in. To this day, people visit her grave, which has been nicknamed "The Witch's Ball." The dense stone ball is said to be uncomfortably warm to the touch, year round, no matter how cold it is outside. No matter how much snow falls in Cleveland, the cursed headstone will always be warm enough to melt the snow collecting on and around the ball. There was also the case of the Johnstown Witch in Licking County, where the public believed that a young girl was a servant of the devil because of her manic fits and her reports of a tall shadow of a man approaching her in her room at night.

Modern-day reports of satanic activity are constantly flowing throughout Licking County Ohio. It is suspected that a cult of witches resides in Johnstown, Ohio, and leave gifts and offerings on the Johnstown Witch's grave. In 2015, in Heath Ohio, a nineteen-year-old girl was injured during a satanic ritual being performed in a cemetery. One night at Mount Calvary Cemetery, a group of young people snuck into the cemetery to perform a satanic ritual. A car drove by, and the young lady, fearing it was the police, took off running to avoid getting caught. As she went running through the dark, she fell down a cliff in the cemetery and became seriously injured. The other cultists who were there that night called for help, and when the police and fire team arrived, the young girl was taken to the Wexner

Medical Center. The police at the scene confirmed that the teens were up to something ritualistic but declined to further explain. It is widely speculated that the group was attempting to tamper with buried remains, and the police declined to speak on it for the privacy of the family of the deceased.

Throughout 2016, the following year, in Newark, Ohio, satanic graffiti started going up all over the city. Signs outside local churches were being changed or painted over to give praise to Satan. Garage doors of private residences were having pentagrams and goat heads spray-painted on them during the night. Residents who lived near the high school reported having the body of headless chickens being left on their doorstep or the hood of their vehicles. Although some of the activity has calmed down since then, people still fear that a cult is in the area, performing rituals and choosing victims from Christian homes to target and torment in the name of the devil. In 2018, in Hebron, Ohio, a private residence reached out to a local paranormal investigation team for help. Apparently, the owner of the house recently started noticing strange activity happening in the home, such as the sound of footsteps in the hallway as she tried to sleep at night, doors opening or closing on their own and vivid, terrifying dreams about being trapped in hell and attempting to escape. During the course of a lengthy investigation, the paranormal team found a small doll made out of twigs and human hair under the doormat on the front porch. Once the item was removed, the house never had another paranormal event reported. The homeowner believes that some type of witch or devil worshipper had placed that doll-like item on her porch to curse her, since she was a very active member of her church.

The Satanic Panic might be slowly dying down as the times change, but that doesn't change the fact that a lot of satanic activity has been happening in the Buckeye State. With new reports of cult-like activity flowing in from Licking County just about every year, it makes you wonder if that panic has any merit to it. Is there a cult in Licking County that is attempting to do the work of the devil? What sort of abilities do these people have, and what can they do to the ones that they target? Or is the Satanic Panic just a manufactured gimmick to try to get people back into the church and scare people into living within traditional Christian values? Hopefully all of the activity that has been on the rise is just a bunch of bored teenagers looking for a way to scare people in their community. Nothing has gotten out of hand just yet, and local law enforcement are actively doing what they can to keep their people safe. According to scripture, the battle between good and evil has been happening for all of time, and it will continue on forever. Let's all hope that nothing that these cults can do is strong enough to tip the scales in the devil's favor.

Poltergeists in Pataskala

A lot of people seem to be slightly confused about what exactly a poltergeist is. The word *poltergeist* is a German word that simply means "noisy spirit." The majority of hauntings that have been investigated and documented in the past are residual hauntings, which usually happens when something so horrible occurs that negative energy is shot off into the atmosphere and creates an imprint on the environment. It creates a sort of recording of time that plays over and over again. These will not be intelligent hauntings, so investigators will not be able to properly interact or communicate with whatever is happening in the home, business or location. These hauntings are also a lot easier to get rid of. If a spirit in a home is free moving, free thinking and able to communicate, then it is considered an intelligent haunting. A poltergeist is pretty different, but they are nothing like how the media depicts them.

A poltergeist isn't some sadistic demonic spirit from the inner pits of hell. Usually, they are just a group of a handful of intelligent spirits that sort of pool their energy together to create more intense activity. A singular intelligent spirit will haunt in a mild manner because it doesn't have a lot of energy to use. Spirits need an energy source in order to manifest or "haunt." The same way that human bodies need to eat food to absorb calories and be able to do work, speak and move, an intelligent spirit will need to drain batteries; feed off psychic energy of anger, sadness or fear; or latch itself on to a spiritually sick or wounded person to use as a source. One intelligent spirit might be able to push a ball very slightly, gently crack a door open, create the sound of footsteps, manifest as a shadow of a human form and hide small objects from residents of the home. With more spirits acting together as a poltergeist, they have more energy to create a more frightening haunting. They can knock as loud as a living being on doors and walls. They can slam doors with force or rip open cabinet drawers and slam them shut. They can pull sheets off a bed, throw or move heavy objects across a room, lift items straight into the air or manifest enough to appear as a fully formed apparition where parts of their appearance can be described in detail.

Poltergeist cases have shown that each scenario is different. The most common poltergeist activity revolves around females in their teen years. Teenage females tend to be very in touch with their emotions, and going through the experience of puberty, when the body is ramping up its production of hormones, can intensify the emotions that they are going through. When negative things happen in a puberty-aged female's life—such as the death of a loved one, changing homes and schools, severe bullying, physical attacks or traumatic assaults or severe depression and suicidal tendencies—then these young women can give off a large beacon of psychic energy. If there are any spirits in the home or surrounding area, they might be attracted to this beacon, and they sort of gather around and follow this person in order to feed off this energy until they are able to manifest. To clarify, teenage women are not the only ones who are able to attract a poltergeist. Any person from any gender, sex, age or background can be the target of a poltergeist; it just seems to happen more commonly with teenagers going through puberty. It should also be known that spirits will not be summoned out of thin air. Most of the spirits involved in a poltergeist were already on the property due to a tragic accident or death that occurred in the past, or they latch on and follow the host from a haunted location that they visited. Poltergeists have also happened to people in completely calm and stable states of mind. All of the activity has been different, and no two cases have been the exact same.

This is why, in nearly every poltergeist case, one person seems to be the main focal point of the haunting. Sometimes the moment this person leaves the house, all activity in the home will cease. Even if a poltergeist is haunting a family in their home, one member of the family will appear to be receiving the worst of it or have all of the activity centered on them. This person might have bruises or visible scars appear on their body, night terrors and a negative shift in personality and appearance. The focal point of the poltergeist most likely has gone through a very stressful or traumatic experience, and once they go through treatment, receive medical care or seek the help of a counselor or psychiatrist, the haunting will die down. If that isn't what clears up the poltergeist, then the next step is to try to appease the spirits. Find the source of their anger and remedy the situation. Sometimes poltergeists spawn when an object with strong emotional attachments to the property is tampered with or disrespected, such as a grave or a photo album. If the offending behavior is corrected, then the poltergeist will be put at ease and leave. Some poltergeist cases have been solved in a few days, others have taken years and some have never been corrected to this day.

Poltergeists have been reported for most of human history, some going as far back as ancient Rome, but one of the most famous and well-documented cases happened in Enfield, England. This is the haunting that inspired the second movie in the Conjuring horror movie franchise. The Conjuring franchise follows the cases of famous paranormal investigators Ed and Lorraine Warren, and the second movie of the series is about the Enfield Poltergeist, despite the fact that the Warrens never actually investigated that case. During their careers, the Warrens were heavily criticized and speculated to be frauds by both skeptics and famously credited paranormal experts. Most of the people they "helped" report that the Warrens arrived unannounced, did nothing to help the victims of the hauntings, antagonized any active spirits in order to make the haunting worse, documented the haunting and its aggressive outbursts and then left to write books and movies about the experience while the family stayed behind to deal with the mess they made. Some of the victims from the Warrens' investigated cases say that the Warrens arrived simply to make a quick buck, but some other people report that the Warrens were actually able to help them and bring their family peace.

The investigator who actually worked on the Enfield Poltergeist case was a journalist and paranormal investigator named Guy Playfair, who just recently passed away in 2018. He published a book about his experience with the poltergeist titled *This House Is Haunted*. Playfair said in an interview about the poltergeist case that Ed and Lorraine Warren arrived to the house and tried to get information about the case from him, and when he wouldn't share much detail, Ed told him that he could help make Playfair rich from books and movie scripts they could write about the activity. Playfair believed that they were not there to actually help the case, but rather to profit off it, and everyone at the scene asked them to leave. Playfair and his investigation team returned to their studies of the activity.

Poltergeist activity was first reported by the family in the home in 1977. The activity started small. The family would hear knocking on the walls and footsteps in the hallway while they were trying to sleep at night. Objects would be moved on their own or go missing. The single mother of the family, Peggy, spoke with the neighbors about the activity, and the neighbors confirmed that they could hear strange noises coming from the home as well. With that knowledge, the mother of the family decided to call the police. Two officers arrived to check on the family and investigate the home for potential intruders. One officer wrote an official report of seeing a chair move roughly four feet completely on its own. As word of the haunting began to spread, news reporters and paranormal investigators began arriving to study the case and attempt to help the family. The main target of the poltergeist seemed to be eleven-year-old Janet Hodgson. Janet disclosed having her bed shaken in the middle of the night and being used as a conduit for the spirit of a previous home owner, Bill Wilkens, to speak through her. It was quite startling to hear the deep, gravelly voice of an elderly man coming out of the mouth of an eleven-year-old.

The activity became more aggressive over the next year and a half. One photographer got hit in the eye by a flying LEGO brick that was thrown entirely on its own. The photographer had a scar from the scratch for several days. Tables were being flipped over, furniture was being dragged around the house, fires would randomly ignite and in one instance, Janet Hodgson was photographed being pulled out of bed and levitating above the floor. Skeptics have criticized the authenticity of this investigation for decades because the girls have admitted to faking a few of the events. In adulthood, Janet admitted that a few events that happened in the house were staged, or done by her or her sister, just to see if the paranormal investigators would be able to catch them. Apparently, the investigators were always able to determine when the events unfolding were not authentic to a haunting. This reassured the family that the investigators were not playing into superstition for entertainment or financial reason but were actually there to help the family deal with what they were going through and rid the poltergeist from the home. The case was never truly solved, but the activity died down. A priest visited the home and did his best to bless the house and put the spirits at rest. The activity became far less intense but did not stop completely, and reports of activity still remain in that house to this day.

Poltergeists are not nearly as common as people might think that they are. It is rare to find a house or business that is truly haunted, and even then, the activity is usually much tamer. However, Licking County, Ohio, and more specifically Pataskala, Ohio, have had quite their fair share of poltergeist activity, which is alarming given how few and far between these events happen. Some victims have gone to paranormal investigation teams for help, and others decided to contact clergy or local psychics who offer their services. Some people going through poltergeist activity have actually handled the situation entirely on their own. A lot of these stories are shared online, so the accuracy and validity of their stories cannot be confirmed, but they sure are fun to read.

One report of poltergeist activity took place at a series of mobile homes or "trailer park" near South Main Street in Pataskala, Ohio. People living in different homes in the community would talk and share experiences of loud and aggressive paranormal activity in their units. Some people had very mild hauntings, such as returning home to lights being on when they were turned off before leaving or doors slowly swinging open on their own with no explanation. Other people had stories of lightweight objects such as kitchen utensils, pet toys, newspapers or magazines and discarded clothing being lifted up and stuck on their ceilings. A few homeowners shared stories of doors being slammed shut when the family was sleeping during the night or kitchen drawers repeatedly opening and closing on their own when people would enter the room. Apparently, a handful of concerned parents contacted a church in the area and had a priest come bless any home that desired it, and the activity died down. It was suspected that the homes were being built or placed over land that used to be a battleground, and the activity was caused when a home was placed over unmarked buried human remains.

Another poltergeist case was reported on Township Road only about a decade ago. Names have been changed to keep anonymity of anyone involved. The target of this poltergeist was a twelve-year-old girl named Jordan. The activity began in a very tame manner. The usual knocking and whispering was reported, and the children of the house actually thought it was cool. One night in the fall, the preteen girl decided to use a Ouija board to try to communicate with the spirits and see what they would need in order to be laid to rest. The lights were turned off, candles were lit and the mood was set to speak with the dead. Nearly a half hour passed with no activity or response to any questions. Jordan gave up, blew out the candles and packed up the board for the night. That night, she reported having a dream that she was standing in the hallway leading to her bedroom, except the stairs leading to that level of the house were missing. The hallway had four walls, no doors or windows and was ominously dark. The entire nightmare was centered on the idea that she couldn't get out of the hallway, panicking as she banged on the walls and yelled for help.

After this dream and the supposed failed Ouija board session, activity in the house picked up dramatically. Jordan would be sleeping at night when her bed would aggressively shake from side to side and wake her up, only to find no one in the room. She, as well as other members of the family, would hear a disembodied voice calling out Jordan's name in a song-like tone from empty rooms throughout the house. As time went on, the poltergeist behind this voice began to manifest more. It started throwing objects at the family while they were gathered in the kitchen eating or relaxing in the living room. A black, mist-shaped mass was seen dashing into rooms or out of sight line when members of the house would turn a corner or suddenly look down the hallway. One night, Jordan had a friend, Amanda, over for a sleepover. The girls were in Jordan's bedroom when they felt the house begin to shake and a loud whistling sound echoed through the house. It was as if a train was passing through their backyard. The girls ran out of the house, but nothing strange was happening outside. Amanda decided that she couldn't sleep in the house after that and went home. Jordan and her family decided to move out of the home. They never found out what was happening in that home.

A home on Graham Road had a brief case of a poltergeist. No activity in the home was reported until the homeowners began talking about remodeling or deconstructing the home. The family brought contractors in for quick estimates on the cost and time frame of some of the work that they wanted done. The next morning, the family emerged from their respective bedrooms to find every single knife they owned, including butter knives, stabbed into the living room floor. Later that day, cabinets in the kitchen began opening and loudly slamming shut when no one was in the room. As the younger son of the family tried to sleep that night, his toys were rolling around his bedroom floor or turning on and activating all by themselves. The family had to apologize out loud to the house and promise that they would not change anything before the activity ceased. No reported hauntings have come from that residence ever since.

Pataskala is a pretty old city, and something must have happened on its soil to create so much aggressive paranormal activity. Many people in the city have some type of ghost story, and it is a running joke that the entire city is haunted. But it baffles most local paranormal researchers that so much paranormal phenomena, of a type usually pretty rare to find, is happening so frequently here. Maybe Licking County residents are just really good at upsetting spirits. If you or anyone you know is experiencing paranormal or poltergeist activity, there are a lot of paranormal investigators, psychic mediums and church officials who are on standby and available to help you. Ohio is such a dark and haunted place that nearly every town in it has a group of people dedicated to helping people with their paranormal problems. Hopefully someday all the poltergeists in Pataskala, Ohio, will be put at ease.

Hitchhike Hauntings

Have you ever been driving along the road and spotted someone walking next to the pavement? It can be nerve-wracking to see a pedestrian that close to the road because it is a dangerous place to be with all the cars going by. People have been hitchhiking for decades now, and it is usually done on low-traffic two-lane roads during the daytime. A lot of car accidents and vehicular manslaughter cases involving hitchhikers happen when someone is walking along a busy road at night time, and they don't seem to be far enough away from traffic. The deaths that have occurred due to people being too close to a busy street or highway are a grave reminder for everyone to be very careful when hitchhiking or to avoid it all together. The dangers of hitchhiking are elevated if you are doing it in Licking County because you wouldn't only be trying to avoid oncoming vehicles, but you might also want to avoid the spirits of those that have been hit in the past. Reports of spirits and ghostly apparitions on the side of the road come in from all over Licking County, and they seem to always be heading in the direction of Newark. Where are all these ghosts coming from?

Hitchhiking has sort of always been around, but it seemed to become much more common during the '60s and '70s, as the hippie lifestyle became more common. Young people were fleeing the establishment and corporations and were challenging the traditional lifestyles of the generations before them. They felt comfortable living nomadic lifestyles full of love and adventures. It was normal to see someone walking alongside the road asking for a ride to the next town over or the nearest music show, and people were comfortable picking these strangers up because most of them were known for their loving and happy personalities. Sometimes hitchhikers would be picked up by other hippies or flower children and join their "family" permanently. The practice of hitchhiking was common for a few years until horror stories of the activity became more frequent. Around this time, the Satanic Panic was setting in, and reports of famous serial killers were flooding in from all over the country. Charles Manson's family committed their murders in 1969. Ted Bundy was claiming victims during the middle years of the '70s. John Wayne Gacy was caught and arrested in 1978. With all of the horrendous crimes coming to light and the sense of danger lurking in every community, people became less interested in traveling with or picking up complete strangers. The case that really cemented the fear of hitchhikers wouldn't come until the next decade, with the case of Aileen Wuornos.

For a whole year between 1989 and 1990, Aileen Wuornos went on a killing spree in Florida. People are still debating whether or not she was a murderous psychopath or a victim herself, but that debate is what caused her case to be highly publicized and catch the media by storm. Aileen lived a very troubled life. She began her escorting and sex work at the young age of eleven years old. She had lost both parents, her father to jail and her mother from abandonment, so she was living with her grandparents. She lost her grandmother soon after being placed in her care, and her grandfather, among the last of her remaining family, was allegedly physically and sexually abusive to her for the majority of her time in his care. She was forced into having a baby for a friend of her grandfather's while she was still a teenager. By the age of fifteen, she had dropped out of school, gave up her son for adoption and ran off to live in the woods because she believed that the wilderness was far safer for her than any home where her grandfather lived.

She hitchhiked her way to Florida, where she made ends meet to survive by prostituting herself and stealing food. She married a wealthy old man in retirement when she was twenty years old, and he reported that she was very abusive to him. After just over two months of marriage, with her beating this man with his own canes and drinking all his money at the local bar, the elderly man filed for divorce and got a restraining order against Wuornos. Her life continued to crumble, as more of her surviving family died and she began getting into more and more trouble from DUIs and drunkenly starting fights in bars she frequented. She started elevating her theft into armed robbery and even got arrested a few times for holding people at gunpoint. Not long after her release, she committed her first murder.

Aileen went on a spree from November 1989 to the end of 1990. She would either hide in the backseat of men's cars to rob and kill them once they entered the vehicle, or she would hitchhike along highways at night and murder men who would pick her up. She changed her story from time to time, saying that she was either trying to rob the men before something went wrong and she had to kill them or that the men were forcing themselves onto her and she was protecting herself. Through the years, she killed six men along Florida's highways and became the tenth woman in the United States to receive the death penalty. The Wuornos case was national news on everyone's TV in the early '90s, and from then on, people immediately associated hitchhikers with murderers. The archetype of a hitchhiking killer has been the premise for scary movies, ghostly stories and urban legends ever since.

Ohio had its own hitchhiking murderer, even though the case wasn't nearly as big as Aileen's was. Michael Beuke was picked up while hitchhiking and murdered a motorist in 1983 in Cincinnati, Ohio, before being arrested and executed as well. Nowadays, picking up a stranger on the side of the road is seen as a ridiculous way to get yourself hurt, and entering a stranger's vehicle is viewed the same way. However, it still happens from time to time, but it is common to hear of those stories going horribly wrong as well. Cases of runaway teenagers or free-spirited young adults hitchhiking away from home, only for their bodies to be found somewhere shortly after, have been popping up all across the nation. It must happen more often than we know of, though, because the roads and highways leading into Newark, Ohio, have so many spirits wandering them.

The most famous road wandering spirit is at the Granville exit on Route 16 East heading into Newark. When drivers turn onto that exit, as an overwhelming number of people have reported, they can see a man standing on the side of the road. He is described as looking lost and confused, and he is wearing an old-fashioned business suit that looks as though it would be from the 1940s. People usually notice him as they are driving by, but when they turn their heads or check the rearview mirrors, no one is standing there. No one knows for sure exactly who the spirit belongs to or what his story is, but there is a theory that most people tend to believe. Years ago, a truck driver went missing from a rest stop, and they found his body not far from that exit. People believe that the spirit might be that truck driver, but it wouldn't explain why he is wearing a business suit and why his spirit is stuck or chooses to haunt a random highway exit. Not a lot has been learned about this spirit, as he is pretty difficult to study. Most paranormal investigators agree that trying to capture haunted activity next to a loud and busy highway won't come up with the best results.

Another popular ghost sighting is on Route 37, on a long stretch of road going from Lancaster, Ohio, into Newark. This route has been nicknamed the "Highway to Heaven" because so many fatal car accidents occur on it every year. Motorists who frequently drive on this highway at nighttime have reported seeing a woman with dark hair wearing a white-lace nightgown or simple dress. This woman might be standing on the side of the road staring at the cars that drive by, or in quite the terrifying fashion, she might casually walk in a relaxed and slow manner across the highway as cars approach her going more than sixty-five miles per hour. Some drivers report slamming on their breaks or swerving into other lanes to avoid hitting this crazy woman, but their vehicle will either pass right through her or she vanishes into thin air right before the car makes contact. This haunting is suspected to be a residual haunting. Seeing as the woman doesn't exactly interact with the environment or give any signs that she has any idea where she is, people think that she is just an apparition of a woman walking through what used to be her house or maybe her garden back in the 1800s but is now an active highway.

On Route 70, the highway that runs through the middle of central Ohio has a wandering spirit problem as well. The stretch of road that goes from Kirksville, past Buckeye Lake and Hebron, Ohio, and toward Zanesville has reports of ghostly children seen on the side of the road. The children seem to be a girl between the age of nine and twelve and a boy between the age of six and eight; they have been spotted in different locations between the lake and Bowling Green Creek. No matter what time of year they are seen, they are always wearing heavy clothing, and they have very pale skin and blue lips and are visibly shivering. People have seen these kids huddled up next to each other sitting on the ground, which has caused more than a few drivers to circle back around after speeding past them, only to find that they have disappeared. Some nighttime drivers have said that the kids were running across the road in the darkness, usually in the direction of a gas station or a fast-food restaurant, but disappear when they reach the other side of the road. Sightings of these kids don't happen too often, but given the nature of their appearance, the main theories for their origin have been theorized. Some people believe that the children might have been homeless or runaways and died from hypothermia during a bad winter. Other people believe that they were murdered kidnap victims and that the shivering motions they make are actually them shaking in fear. They are running across the highway to get away from their abductors, even now in the afterlife.

Another child spirit is reported in Alexandria, Ohio, on Mounts Road. When people are walking near the bike trail, the apparition of a little girl has been seen running across the road. She will be heading from down the hill, into the ditch on the other side of the pavement, and then disappear. People have noticed that she seems to be heading toward the direction of the cemetery, not far from the trail. There is a lot of speculation about who this girl is, but people really hope that she isn't the spirit of a child who was killed and had her body buried somewhere on the path.

The network of roads and highways in Licking County might have seen a lot more tragedy and heartbreak than we are aware of. Looking at all the ghost sightings and urban legends, such as Swamp Road Sallie, it seems like you can't drive for longer than ten minutes without encountering a spirit of some kind. Not to mention the number of unsolved murders and mysteries that might have happened on the side of our highways were never solved—the bodies of these restless spirits have never been recovered. If you find yourself traveling in or out of Newark anytime soon, try to avoid stopping for the strangers on the side of the road. That stranger that you pull over to help might just disappear into thin air. Or even worse, they could be a dangerous serial killer, looking to claim a kind driver as their next victim.

Spring Valley Nature Preserve

The Spring Valley Nature Preserve is a beautiful forty-five-acre property in southern Granville that is open for the public to use. The preserve has multiple walking trails leading off the main trail for Granville locals to take their pets, shelters to hold gatherings and birthday parties and wide-open fields for playing games. All of the trails are marked, and you can find maps showing how long the trails go. According to the Granville Recreation District, the Licking Land Trust obtained the property in 2007 and has opened the area up to the public ever since. The area around the nature preserve holds a few businesses and houses, and people who work or live in the area will be the first to tell you that the entire area is full of paranormal activity. Spring Valley has so many spirits inside of it, and some of the homes that sit on or close to the property have issues with the ghosts of the preserve haunting their residence as well.

Basically, all of Granville, Ohio, is one big paranormal hot spot, but a lot of the private residences that have paranormal activity are the ones near the preserve. While in their homes, people have reported seeing the apparition of a young girl and a middle-aged man. Sometimes they will appear together, either walking through people's yards or standing in their hallways. Other times they manifest individually. They seem to be intelligent spirits because witnesses report that they watch the residents of the home when they sleep or do chores around the house. One resident, a paranormal researcher herself, was able to use flashlights and a REM pod to get the spirits to communicate with her. This particular pair of spirits seems to be friendly and unintentionally scare the people they observe with the sound of their footsteps moving through their home or by moving objects that the homeowners will notice later.

Spring Valley Nature Preserve is believed to be home to an earth elemental or haunted by a group of Granville's Civil War veterans.

Other spirits reported in the area don't seem so nice. Another resident of a home on the preserve's property reported physical contact by the spirit of an older woman. She will scratch the guests who visit the house and has knocked glasses and mugs full of liquids off the counter and onto the floor. A lot of homes in the area also report aggressive voices, seemingly arguing with one another, coming out of rooms that are completely empty. People hear disembodied cries and groans throughout their house, and one person actually heard a woman screaming and wailing coming from the preserve as they were trying to fall asleep.

While walking the trails of the preserve, people have experienced even more unexplainable activity. A girl wearing a settler's style of dress and head bonnet is seen peeking out from around trees pretty often. Some pictures taken during birthday parties or family gatherings at the preserve have captured images of her watching the event go on. Voices echo through the property, calling for help or crying that they are hurt, but when hikers run to the source of the sound to investigate, no one is there. Joggers who run through the area have reported instances where they would arrive at the reserve in perfect health and take a thirty-minute jog along the trails where no branches or vines were near the path, but they will still find scratches or claw marks on their backs or arms when they would return to their car. It seems like the spirits that inhabit the wooded parts of the preserve are more protective of their environment.

People have brought in mystics to sage their homes or hang mistletoe, frankincense and myrrh throughout their house in an attempt to ward off evil spirits. No matter what is done to try to get rid of the spirits and the frightening paranormal activity in the area, the phenomena continue. The spirits here will not let go of the land, and that has raised many questions about who they are and why they are still here. From all the investigating that has happened so far, there are two main theories as to what is causing the hauntings.

Granville has seen a little bit of conflict during its history. During the Civil War, there was a not so well-known battle known as the Battle of North Mountain that was mostly fought in northeast West Virginia. The 135th Ohio Volunteer Army was the main force that was fighting for the Union, and these troops faced massive casualties. This particular army mostly consisted of recruits from Licking County. Thirty-two of the soldiers were from Granville, and seventeen of them were captured by the enemy. Being captured by the Confederate army was worse than dying on the battlefield to them. These soldiers were stripped of all their possessions, including their boots. They were forced to march, barefoot, for a week through the hills of Virginia, where most of them died from exhaustion, heat stroke or illnesses. The survivors were put into a cattle car to be shipped to the South. The remaining soldiers were barely given food and water, and they were crammed into the tiny car with almost no room to move or stretch.

The eight-day trip to Georgia in unsanitary and uncomfortable conditions caused all of them to get sick. When they arrived in Georgia, they were placed in a prisoner of war camp with other captives from the Union army. They spent their remaining days in a field without shade, water, almost no food and a lack of medical care. These death camps were grueling and, at one point, were witnessing one hundred Union prisoner deaths per day. The soldiers were able to write letters to their family and Union reinforcements back home, but the Union and Confederacy did not have a prisoner exchange agreement in place. The prisoner of war camp in Andersonville, Georgia, was too well secured and deep in the South that leading a liberation would be too challenging to risk. Nothing could be done to save the Granville prisoners. The men of the 135th Ohio Volunteer Army were brave warriors. The unit was assembled in 1864 in Columbus from members of Licking County's National Guard. Out of 2,919 men living in Granville or attending Denison University, more than 600 of them served in the Civil War. Nearly all of the men who fought in the Battle of North Mountain died in battle, did not survive the hike to Virginia or were worked to death in Georgia. Of the soldiers who died, about 5 of them lived in southern Granville, with their parents' homes being not too far away from the land that now forms the Spring Valley Nature Preserve.

Some people believe that the hauntings on the property belong to the spirits of these soldiers. Since their deaths were very traumatic, their spirits might have been trying to find their way home but got lost in the foliage in Granville. These spirits might be wandering the woods, confusing it for the terrain that they were torturously marched through after their capture.

Other people don't believe this theory, as the soldiers would not be scratching people who jogged by. It also doesn't explain where the children and the old woman spirit came from or why these soldiers would be heard fighting in the homeowner's living rooms.

The alternative theory to what is causing the hauntings is that the spirits in the woods are elementals, not ghosts. An elemental is a nature spirit or guardian that is usually closely attached to one of the four elements. They have never walked the earth in a human form and are usually spawned from different dimensions or manifest from the results of a tragedy or environmental destruction. An example of a water elemental would be an undine, or a water-born spirit, protecting an old lighthouse or haunting communities of beach houses that are polluting the area. Fire elementals tend to be born out of fire-based tragedy, such as a hospital being burned down with many casualties. If the hospital is repaired or torn down for a new building to be constructed, a fire elemental may haunt the area. Earth elementals, which is what is thought to be haunting Spring Valley, are usually fairies or gnomes.

Most professional paranormal investigators don't believe in elementals, and neither does the general public. They are seen as stories from mythology and can't possibly be real. However, stories of elementals have been around for a long time. For example, many Native American tribes worshiped these nature spirits before the European colonists arrived. Many practicing shamans of the tribes would share stories of their training or apprenticeship that would involve going into nature and working with the nature spirits. Elementals have been investigated, just like ghosts and poltergeists. The most famous elemental case in the world was reported at Leap Castle in Ireland. The castle was constructed in the early thirteenth century and has seen countless battles and wars during its lifetime. The interior of the castle has seen just as much bloodshed as the exterior, with trapdoors leading to a floor of deadly spikes being used to execute people throughout the castle. Hundreds of people have died in the castle, either from battle, execution, disease or even murder. One documented case shares a story of a man murdering his brother in the chapel of the castle to take his spot in line for the throne.

Through all the death and destruction of the property, an evil elemental spawned in the shadows of Leap Castle. The elemental was named "It" and "The Thing" by the first person to ever witness It, Mildred Dill. Mildred and her family moved into the castle in 1889, after centuries of horrors had happened in the castle. She wrote about her first encounter with It in her diary. Mildred described that she was standing in the gallery, looking down at the main floor, when something touched her shoulder. She turned to look at who grabbed her and was horrified to find the vilest creature she had ever seen. It was the size of a sheep with a human, yet inhuman, face. It had black cavities for eyes that stared back into hers and a thin, decrepit body. The Thing gave off a horrible smell of rotting flesh and decay that was strong enough to choke a man to death. Mildred wrote of a second time that she saw the Thing, this time with her husband. When they heard other people in the castle scream and run down the hall, Mildred and her husband ran out of their bedroom to see what was happening. With her husband in front of her, they entered the gallery to see It, leaning over the handrails and staring down onto the main floor at the employees. As they looked at It, with the smell of death and decay filling the room, it slowly vanished into thin air.

Paranormal teams from all over the world have journeyed to Leap to investigate the famous elemental. The castle is viciously haunted by dozens upon dozens of human spirits, and occasionally, teams will be unlucky enough to catch a glimpse of the death elemental known as It. It is suspected that the elemental manifested from the negative energy around the castle, and with so much death and decay seeping into the walls of the building and the soil of the property, part of that death was picked up and used in the creation of the elemental.

Those who believe in the existence of elementals are firm in their theory that an earth elemental is inside the Spring Valley Nature Preserve. The spirit might only be scratching people on the trails who accidentally threaten it, and it is just trying to protect the land from anyone who might cause the foliage harm. Elemental spirits typically aren't negative or dangerous, so that theory would not explain why so many other spirits are trapped on the property. Elementals are not known for trapping human spirits in a confined area, and they also wouldn't be screaming and wailing into the night, as so many people have reported hearing.

Whatever is happening in Spring Valley, it is definitely the work of the supernatural. The woods surrounding the beautiful walking trails are inhabited by the spirits of Civil War veterans or by a frightened elemental that is trying its best to protect its home. Or maybe both theories are wrong and the preserve needs more investigators to check out the area to see what they can discover. It is highly suggested that Ohio nature lovers check out Spring Valley Nature Preserve at some point in time, but if you are planning on going, please be respectful of the environment. It might save you from a scratch or two.

Bibliography

Associated Press. "Deputy Says Union County Is a Satanic Center." April 15, 1985. https://apnews.com/d7221d0cca4265edb63afe91e7b892ae.

Bennett, B.K. "A Bitter Pill: Granville and the Battle of North Mountain, July 3rd, 1864." *Historical Times*, 2011.

Bruner, B. "Police: 1 Falls Off Cemetery Cliff After 'Satanic Ritual.'" *Newark Advocate*, June 23, 2015. https://www.newarkadvocate.com/story/news/local/2015/06/23/woman-flown-hospital-heath-cemetery-fall/29147815.

Bryn Du Commission. "Our History." Retrieved October 30, 2021. https://www.bryndu.com/our-history.

Commencement of the Ohio Canal at the Licking Summit, July 4, 1825. Columbus, OH: F.J. Heer Printing Company, 1926.

Correia, Z. "The Legacy of Denison's Cemetery and Its Famous Alumnus." The Denisonian, November 5, 2019. https://denisonian.com/2019/10/features/the-legacy-of-denisons-cemetery-and-its-famous-alumnus.

The Denisonian. "The History of the Buxton Inn: Is It Really Haunted?" November 5, 2019. Retrieved November 23, 2021 https://denisonian.com/2019/10/features/the-history-of-the-buxton-inn-is-it-really-haunted.

Denison University. "Our History." Retrieved October 23, 2021. https://denison.edu/campus/about/our-history.

Explore Ohio Outdoors. "Spring Valley Nature Preserve." November 2, 2021. https://www.exploreohiooutdoors.com/post/spring-valley-nature-preserve.

Gebhart, D. "The Chieftain Wacousta, the Young Lahkopis, and the Maiden Ahyomah." *Ohio History Journal*. Retrieved October 8, 2021. https://resources.ohiohistory.org/ohj/search/display.php?page=77&ipp=20&searchterm=Array&vol=13&pages=455-457.

Granville Inn—Granville, Ohio. "The History of the Granville Inn." Retrieved October 30, 2021. https://granvilleinn.com/the-history-of-the-granville-inn.

Granville Recreation District. "Spring Valley." Retrieved November 25, 2021. https://www.granvillerec.org/parks-facilities/spring-valley.

Guglielmi, J. "Inside the Real Story that Inspired the Conjuring 2." *People*, June 10, 2016. https://people.com/movies/inside-the-real-story-that-inspired-the-conjuring-2.

Haines, G.K. "CIA's Role in the Study of UFOs, 1947–90." FAS Project on Government Secrecy. Retrieved November 28, 2021. https://sgp.fas.org/library/ciaufo.html.

Haunted Rooms America. "Historic Buxton Inn, Granville, Ohio." June 10, 2021. https://www.hauntedrooms.com/most-haunted-hotels-in-america#ohio.

Hedges, A. "Black-Eyed Kids: The Chilling Legend that Began in Abilene." Texas Hill Country, July 12, 2019. https://texashillcountry.com/black-eyed-kids-legend-abilene.

Jackson, J. "Vandals Wanted for Obscene Graffiti on Newark Church, Homes." WSYX, May 3, 2016. https://abc6onyourside.com/news/local/vandals-wanted-for-obscene-graffiti-on-newark-church-homes.

Johnstown, Ohio. "History of Johnstown, Ohio." Retrieved October 4, 2021. https://johnstownohio.org/history.

Licking County. "Sheriff's Department History." Retrieved October 2, 2021. https://lickingcounty.gov/depts/sheriff/sheriffs_history.htm.

Licking County Historic Jail. "History." June 20, 2019. https://lcjail.org/history-of-the-old-licking-county-jail.

Licking County Library's Wiki. "Licking County Jail." Retrieved October 6, 2021. http://wiki.lickingcountylibrary.info/Licking_County_Jail.

———. "Murders and Homicides." October 31, 2017. http://wiki.lickingcountylibrary.info/Murders_and_Homicides.

Lincoln Financial Foundation Collection. "Abraham Lincoln Accounts of the Assassination—Surnames S-Z." Retrieved October 12, 2021. http://livinghistoryofillinois.com/pdf_files/Abraham-Lincoln-Accounts-of-the-Assassination-Surnames-S-Z.pdf.

Linder, D.O. "The West Memphis Three Trials: An Account." Famous Trials. Retrieved November 15, 2021 https://famous-trials.com/westmemphis/2287-home.

Lost & Found Ohio Galleries. "Paranormal Investigations / Old Licking County Jail." Retrieved October 5, 2021. http://www.lostandfoundohio.com/gallery/index.php?%2Fcategory%2F403.

Lyon, M. "Leap Castle Is the Most Haunted Castle in Ireland and This Story Proves It." Irish Central, October 31, 2019. https://www.irishcentral.com/roots/history/leap-castle-ghost-story.

Newark Leader. "The Vanishing Canal." April 26, 1934.

Newkirk, G. "Enfield Poltergeist Investigator Says Warrens Never Involved in 'Conjuring 2' Case." Week in Weird, June 9, 2016. http://weekinweird.com/2016/01/07/conjuring-truth-original-enfield-poltergeist-investigator-says-ed-and-lorraine-warren-never-investigated-the-case.

New York Times. "2 Brothers in Ohio Deny Charges in Slaying of 3 by .22-Caliber Gun." January 7, 1979. https://www.nytimes.com/1979/01/07/archives/2-brothers-in-ohio-deny-charges-in-slaying-of-3-by-22caliber-gun.html.

Ohio Department of Natural Resources. "Blackhand Gorge State Nature Preserve." Retrieved October 8, 2021. https://ohiodnr.gov/wps/portal/gov/odnr/go-and-do/plan-a-visit/find-a-property/blackhand-gorge-state-nature-preserve.

Ohio History Central. "Blackhand Gorge State Nature Preserve." Retrieved November 23, 2021. https://ohiohistorycentral.org/w/Blackhand_Gorge_State_Nature_Preserve.

———. "Licking County." Retrieved October 1, 2021. https://ohiohistorycentral.org/w/Licking_County.

PocketSights Tour Builder. "The Captain's Ghost." Licking County Library. Retrieved October 15, 2021. https://pocketsights.com/tours/place/The-Captain%27s-Ghost-51557:5999.

Press, T.A. "Woman Who Killed 6 Is Executed in Florida." *New York Times*, October 10, 2002. https://www.nytimes.com/2002/10/10/us/woman-who-killed-6-is-executed-in-florida.html.

Romano, A. "Why Satanic Panic Never Really Ended." Vox, March 31, 2021. https://www.vox.com/culture/22358153/satanic-panic-ritual-abuse-history-conspiracy-theories-explained.

Saavedra, J. "The Conjuring 2's Enfield Case: A True Story that Still Haunts Us Today." Den of Geek, February 27, 2021. https://www.

denofgeek.com/movies/the-conjuring-2-enfield-case-true-story-janet-bill-wilkins-tape.

Satterfield, J. "The Case of Notorious Murderess Laura Devlin." *Newark Advocate*, September 5, 2015. https://www.newarkadvocate.com/story/news/local/newarks-history/2015/09/05/case-notorious-murderess-laura-devlin/71775136.

St. Jacob's Cemetery Association. "About." Retrieved October 8, 2021. https://stjacobscemetery.org/About.

Stamper, C. "Haunted Newark Walking Tour—The Captain's Ghost." October 26, 2003. Retrieved October 12, 2021. https://www.lickingcountylibrary.org/media/1075/haunted-newark-walking-tour.pdf.

Stockton, R. "How Aileen Wuornos Became History's Most Terrifying Female Serial Killer." All That's Interesting, November 4, 2021. https://allthatsinteresting.com/aileen-wuornos.

Todack, S. "Meeting the People of the 1910 Lynching." The General Idea. Retrieved October 2, 2021. https://thegeneralidea.org/7844/blog/meeting-the-people-of-the-1910-lynching.

Touring Ohio. "Ohio & Erie Canal System." Retrieved October 15, 2021. http://touringohio.com/day-trips/ohio-erie-canal.html.

Weird U.S. "Cedar Hill Cemetery—Weird Ohio." Retrieved October 8, 2021. http://www.weirdus.com/states/ohio/cemetery_safari/cedar_hill_cemetery/index.php.

About the Author

Nova Stiles began investigating urban legends at only fourteen years old, and after a frightening experience at a cemetery in Akron, he became obsessed with the paranormal. In 2021, Nova joined the Tri-C Ghost Hunters, the largest paranormal team in Ohio. He now explores famous haunted locations as well as private residences throughout the country with a team of experts. Nova and the Tri-C Ghost Hunters, the resident paranormal team of the Ohio State Reformatory, teach new investigators how to hunt ghosts at the most haunted jail in America. *Ghosts & Legends of Licking County* is his first book.